Brief Gestalt Therapy

Brief Therapies Series

Series Editor: Stephen Palmer
Associate Editor: Gladeana McMahon

Focusing on brief and time-limited therapies, this series of books is aimed at students, beginning and experienced counsellors, therapists and other members of the helping professions who need to know more about working with the specific skills, theories and practices involved in this demanding but vital area of their work.

Books in the series:

Solution-Focused Therapy
Bill O'Connell

A Psychodynamic Approach to Brief Counselling and Psychotherapy
Gertrud Mander

Brief Cognitive Behaviour Therapy
Berni Curwen, Stephen Palmer and Peter Ruddell

Solution-Focused Groupwork
John Sharry

Brief NLP Therapy
Ian McDermott and Wendy Jago

Transactional Analysis Approaches to Brief Therapy
Keith Tudor

Handbook of Solution-Focused Therapy
edited by Bill O'Connell and Stephen Palmer

Brief Gestalt Therapy

Gaie Houston

SAGE Publications
London • Thousand Oaks • New Delhi

To all those people I have worked with directly, and the many others who come to me for supervision of brief therapy, my thanks for all you have taught me.

First published 2003

SAGE Publications Ltd
6 Bonhill Street
London EC2A 4PU

SAGE Publications Inc
2455 Teller Road
Thousand Oaks, California 91320

SAGE Publications India Pvt Ltd
B-42, Panchsheel Enclave
Post Box 4109
New Delhi 100 017

British Library Cataloguing in Publication data

A catalogue record for this book is available from the British Library

ISBN 0 7619 7348 6
ISBN 0 7619 7349 4 (pbk)

Library of Congress Control Number available

Typeset by C&M Digitals (P) Ltd, Chennai, India
Printed in Great Britain by TJ International Ltd, Padstow, Cornwall

Contents

1
Overview

This book sets out to describe how Gestalt Therapy can be used to good purpose and with good outcomes, in brief interventions with a broad range of variously distressed people. It is aimed at psychotherapy students, and experienced practitioners from other disciplines, who want to feel confident about integrating some of what is explained here, into their approach.

Lack of money from funding bodies is behind much of the current interest in brief methods. That is likely to be a bad reason for adopting any therapeutic style. However, this bad reason may have led, or be leading, towards good therapy.

More than a few people still wait to be convinced that brief therapy can achieve anything worthwhile. Many practitioners and schools stress the value of long-term, and alongside that, are dubious about brief work. Further research is arguably needed to establish whether it is valid to assume very readily that long-term therapy is necessarily more effective than that lasting only a few weeks. The efficacy of short-term work is well evidenced by Bloom (1992). Talmon (1990) argues, yet more radically, that most people who drop out of therapy even after just one session do so because they feel they have been helped enough already.

For many people, brief, rather than rigidly time-limited therapy, is indeed enough (Roth and Fonagy, 1996). For others, whose distress perhaps dates back furthest and is profound, years rather than weeks are certainly needed for the de-construction of old perceptions, and the learning of a new and at best a more rewarding way of living. Even here, there is evidence that brief intervention can be of use; Fisch and Schlanger (1998) describe such work with alcoholism, paranoia, delusion and severe depression, under the appropriate title, *Brief Therapy with Intimidating Cases*. Klerman et al. (1984) describe a brief treatment model successful with moderate and severe depression, based on Sullivan's interpersonal method, analogous to Gestalt dialogic method.

The idea that people can be helped on the road to healing or change through short exposure to therapy is indeed not new.

> There is a great deal of fairly subtle data to support the notion that every human being, if he is not too tediously demoralised by a long series of disasters, comes fairly readily to manifest processes which tend to improve his efficiency as a human being, his satisfactions, and his success in living. (Sullivan, 1954: 100)

The development of brief therapy

In the second half of the twentieth century Cognitive Analytic Therapy and other successful brief methods were developed, often with a borrowing of, or coincidence of invention with, Gestalt ways of working (Flegenheimer, 1982).

Then less attention was paid to the topic in some schools until the millennium approached. In recent years, as we have seen, fund-holders dictate the dosage rate of therapy, often a lower one than their own advisers recommend (Department of Health, 2001). Clinicians trained in careful and painstaking long-term work have needed to adapt, in surgeries and EAP schemes, to what can be seen as the high art form of brief therapy. For some this is a difficult challenge, and one that merits having the principles involved in it spelled out with some care.

Which brand is best?

The aim of any therapy is arguably to enable people to understand and befriend themselves and others, or cope, or move on more rewardingly in their lives. The aim of therapists is at best to be effective in promoting that change. If there is to be a fight between orthodoxy and effectiveness, in any approach, my earnest hope is that effectiveness would win. My experience is that orthodoxy more often does. Then not only effectiveness, but the person who sought help, are victims of the fight.

There is at the moment, nevertheless, some movement towards the integration of approaches to psychotherapy in general. An exchange, sometimes overt, and sometimes a quiet poaching, of theory and methods, is happening between many schools of therapy.

Dialogue, for instance, once claimed as particular to Gestalt, is now used in other approaches too. Transference, a concept central to psychoanalytic work, has now entered the thinking of many humanistic schools. What is clear is that Gestalt arguably offers a very clear rationale and philosophy for integration.

Gestalt Therapy is integrative in its nature. Of all brand-name therapies, it may be seen as one highly suited in its holism for use in brief counselling. A Gestalt practitioner is required to stay alive to, and make sense of, all the data she perceives. If she does this honestly and openly, she cannot close her mind to the perceptions of other schools of therapy. In 1951, before Integrative Therapy was generally spoken of, *Gestalt Therapy* contained the lines:

> In this book we candidly accept as powerful approaches a number of different theories and techniques; they are relevant in the total field, and however incompatible they may seem to their several proponents, they must nevertheless be compatible if one allows the synthesis among them to emerge by acceptance

> and free conflict – for we do not see that the best champions are either stupid or in bad faith, and since we work in the same world, there must somewhere be a creative unity. (Perls et al., 1951: 254)

In terms of both method and theory, then, Gestalt is here seen as a universal or umbrella psychotherapy, which requires the therapist to introduce whatever, in the field of the particular moment created with the particular person, enters her awareness as likely to tend towards effective therapy.

Width of application

Brief therapy is a great test of any method and practitioner. Some schools respond to the hazards of brief intervention by treating only people with particular difficulties, such as phobias or depression. If they do this effectively, it would seem a good idea to think of incorporating their ways of working into other therapies.

There are no standard clients who put themselves forward for short episodes of therapy. A common factor for some will be that they have been referred by a general practitioner. Others will have arrived in the consulting room via an employer scheme. Neither of these factors has very much to do with predicting the sort of distress they are likely to be in.

> ... It is absurd to think even for a moment of not combating the resistances, of not rousing anxiety, of not showing that a neurotic response does not work, of not reviving the past, of withholding all interpretation and discarding one's science.... What is the reality of an interview in which one of the partners, the therapist, inhibits his best power, what he knows and therefore evaluates? (Perls et al., 1951: 286)

This bold statement might seem daunting in the demands it implies on the therapist. It might sceptically be seen as an invitation for a kind of anything-goes approach to therapy. Contradictory theory is generally seen as a poor foundation for good psychotherapy, and eclectic methods imply eclectic theory. Coherence of approach is arguably of great importance in providing a rationale for the understanding of everyone involved (From, 1984).

The contribution of Gestalt

The case for brief therapy is in my view unassailable. To understand more of the contribution Gestalt makes here, we need to go back to its origins. **The aim of Gestalt Therapy is to awaken or mobilise people enough for them to get on better with their lives than they were managing before coming for help**.

> What the doctor sets in motion the patient continues on his own. The 'successful case' upon discharge is not a 'cure' in the sense of being a finished product,

> but a person who now has tools and equipment to deal with problems as they arise. (Perls et al., 1951: 15)

This book will describe a range of Gestalt responses which seem likely to be of use to the many different people who arrive for brief therapy. The emphasis will be, in the words of Paul's (1967) dictum, on **what treatment, by whom, is most effective for this individual with that specific problem, and under which set of circumstances**. In Gestalt language, explained more fully in the following chapter, this means a respectful attention to **context** as well as to **contact**.

> In BGT (Brief Gestalt Therapy), the breadth of possible interventions can be as great as the knowledge of the therapist. This knowledge will be tempered by her judgement of what might best serve this person in this context with this difficulty.

This raises an important question. How rigid are the boundaries within which a Gestalt therapist may work? The contemporary answer is there in the early theory. Fritz Perls, perhaps the best-known early writer on the subject, was a trained and practising psychoanalyst. In the course of developing his radically new approach to psychotherapy, he never lost sight of the value of both psychoanalysis and other approaches.

In his preface to the 1945 edition of *Ego, Hunger and Aggression*, Perls (1992) wrote, with great relevance to now: 'At present there are many "Psychologies", and every school is, at least in part, right. But, alas, every school is also righteous'. (p. xiii) He speaks of the need for integration: 'I have attempted to show that something of this nature can be done, if one throws bridges across the gaps, and I can only hope to stimulate hundreds of other psychologists, psychoanalysts, psychiatrists etc to do the same'. (p. xiii)

The philosopher Karl Popper is clear that the task of scientific enquiry is to work to disprove the accepted truths of the moment. As therapists we deal with the dementingly multivariable, multifactorial, recognisable but not measurable entities that are humans in action and relation. Perhaps this complexity nudges us away from trying to disprove our theories. It is more comfortable to hold on to what seems clear explanation from our teachers and textbooks. Sometimes we grasp an alliterative jingle, or a numbered set of 'stages' or issues designed partly to make us feel safe and competent. Or we may fall back on a couple of maxims uttered by a familiar guru, which seem to justify or inform our work.

Gestalt Therapy is not amenable to formulae, to being manualised in the way that earns plaudits from certain kinds of academic researchers.

The following is a list of the underlying assumptions that characterise Gestalt Therapy, and which, seen as a cluster, an organised whole, distinguish it from others:

1. Gestalt formation

The German word *gestalt* translates roughly to mean *pattern*, *form*, or *organisation*. In this context a gestalt is a field of data, organised by the need of the person experiencing it, into a **figure** or foreground, and a context or **background**. In a crude example, someone just setting up house is likely suddenly to notice the furniture shops he has often passed before unknowingly. They have become **foreground** or **figure** for him in a **gestalt formation** or organising of his way of perceiving what is there. One therapeutic consequence of this assumption about how people organise perception, has strong diagnostic implications. It is a move away from very bounded notions of causality. It stresses that all our experience is formed by a web of interdependent factors. Even this description is insufficient, since it reifies, or makes things, out of what are in reality dynamic flowing experience. The uniqueness of any one person's way of experiencing is valued in this therapy, over and above categorical description.

2. Organisation of the field of perception

Another assumption alongside all the above, is of the dynamic nature of gestalt formation. A central understanding in Gestalt Therapy is that **the dominant need organises the field of perception** of the client.

In other words, people are constantly changing, in terms of their perception, as well as more obviously in their context. This change can be related to a cycle of experience that at best will lead to a resolution or new laying to rest of whatever was figural, and the learning it led to.

Malan was among the first proponents of brief therapy to stress the value of focus on one issue. This in Gestalt theory would be seen as the dominant need. His descriptions of how he works are analogous to the Gestalt approach of staying alert to contact, to just what goes on between therapist and client, and using that as the diagnostic tool. Such overlaps between Gestalt and other methods and theories is a reassurance, perhaps, that there are not vast numbers of good ideas in the world. Those that exist are likely to be used, perhaps dressed in slightly different uniforms, by many schools that can show successful therapeutic outcomes. (Curwen et al., 2000: 3–4, writing about CBT, have many overlaps with BGT.)

3. Holism rather than categories

Rather than list anxiety, depression and so forth as conditions that might be helped by brief therapy, in Gestalt terms it is more congenial to say that many **people** are well served by it. Most neurotic conditions are subject to the spirit of the times. Hysteria has lost its league-table position as a manifestation of distress. Neurasthenia is seldom spoken of now, though even in 1951 Perls still made mention of it. It is strongly arguable that looking at the neurotic manifestation as figure is a distortion of the field. The co-morbidities, the social conditions, all that which adds up to this person now seems the proper figure to address. Gestalt places more emphasis on the individual as a field phenomenon, than on diagnostic categories.

A footnote to this critique of over-dependence on categorical thinking is to use another Gestalt notion, that of polarities, to point out that in English we have invented few balancing constructs to the pathological ones so often mentioned in current writing on the topic. There is not a clear term to denote the opposite of neurosis. In psychotherapeutic theory, there are few specific categories to describe the different forms of wellbeing that the soul, the psyche, may enjoy, even when there is distress in other areas. I use this observation as another argument against thinking in terms of categorical, rather than in personal, subjective and intersubjective description.

The larger aspect of wholism, or holism, that is respected in Gestalt is described in its own jargon as the indivisibility of organism and environment. In something nearer English, this means that nothing, or no one, is truly separable from context. This concept, described at greater length in the next chapter, is perhaps quantitatively rather than qualitatively different from the assumptions in other schools of therapy. It is given great weight in Gestalt.

4. Co-operation

> The problem of psychotherapy is to enlist the patient's powers of creative adjustment without forcing it into the stereotype of the therapist's scientific conception. (Perls et al., 1951: 281)

The therapist may know more about Gestalt, or dialogue, or desirable conditions in therapy, than does the client or group. The people who come for treatment are world authorities on their own perception, have enough health and coping ability, whatever their distress, to have got them this far in their lives and motivated them to seek help. In Gestalt there is stress on recognising the contribution of all parties to the process of therapy. It is not a treatment done to a passive client by an undisclosing expert. The aim is to achieve a horizontal dialogue, with all parties on a level, where the differences between them are perceived as good therapeutic data, and as building blocks.

All successful therapy requires co-operation. It is listed here because Gestalt puts a specially heavy emphasis on this as a condition of the work.

5. Techniques

Gestalt uses the **phenomenological method**. This involves the therapist staying open all the time to the impact on her of the group or person with whom she is working. From this awareness she may comment on what she is experiencing. A client, for example, tells of a recent bereavement, and the therapist replies: 'I am feeling a sort of shock at the sudden death you tell. At the same time, I notice your smile and quick way of talking, and I am uneasy. I need to be slower, somehow, to take in something so large'.

The client acknowledges this speediness. She sees that she has been coping for her whole family by being brisk, and recognises her own need to slow down.

The therapist has not interpreted the data she notices, but has reported on its effect on her and on the **between**, the effect passing back and forth between the two people in the room.

The other major technique is termed **experimentation**. In this context the word covers a multitude of devices that may be invented by clients or therapist. These may be in the service of discovering more about the present, of unlearning old habits or finding new behaviours, about resolving internal conflicts, and much besides.

So part of the aim of this book is to increase the therapist's general skill and repertoire of responses, rather than prescribe just what is to be done when.

6. Dogma or dilution

Divergent schools of practice have developed within Gestalt, as in other major schools, notably psychoanalysis. As there, different developments tend to be defended by their proponents, against all comers. In Gestalt, however, there is some clear common ground. The integrating ideas that at best characterise any sub-divisions of Gestalt theory are to do with:

1. Respecting and raising awareness of the process of gestalt formation itself. This assumes that the individual is indivisible from the context;
2. Assuming a tendency towards autonomy and growth, via a process of gestalt formation and the learning or assimilation intrinsic to it;
3. Looking for the subjective truth of what is going on in the moment for all parties;
4. Relating that truth to the context or background that has led to the present perceptions;
5. Emphasising the autonomy or self-responsibility of the client;
6. Keeping in awareness and commenting on what is often and clumsily called intersubjectivity, the effect of each on the other.

These assumptions form much of what can be likened to the slowly changing river banks, the boundaries through which the content of every BGT therapeutic episode flows, with its varied process and emphasis according to client and practitioner. They dictate dialogic humility on the part of the therapist. Readers will perhaps add other containing ideas important to them. Keeping a simple list of what are nearest to invariable boundaries is useful in the width of innovative experimentation advocated here in BGT.

General psychotherapeutic theory and Gestalt

In recent years there has been a general move to integrate the findings from different disciplines into what may in time become nearer a Gestalt science as well as an art of psychotherapy. The holistic and inclusive intentions of Gestalt are arguments for allowing into it a constant flow of improved understandings, as streams feed a river. New findings in the social sciences, in psychiatry, neurology and philosophy, are a few of the allied disciplines through which Gestalt can both change and maintain itself in the ever-changing present, as any psychotherapy needs to do.

People seem to be helped by many different psychotherapeutic and counselling approaches, from psychodynamic to person-centred to cognitive-behavioural and a host besides. In the light of this we may need to be prepared to adapt our practices, so that we keep effectiveness rather than purism as an outcome criterion. There are many lists of factors deemed to be curative or therapeutic.

Frank (1973) suggests that all therapy, irrespective of the particular approach, produces favourable effects if the following conditions are in place:

1. An emotionally-charged and confiding relationship between healer and sufferer;
2. A healing setting;
3. The arousal of hope;
4. Encouraging changed behaviour outside the session;
5. Encouraging new ways of understanding oneself through corrective emotional experiences;
6. A conceptual scheme or myth to explain symptoms;
7. A ritual to help resolve symptoms.

This description is broad enough that it may take in conversations with priests and philosophers and wise friends, as well as therapists. Readers will add their own notions of what they believe produces change, and thus is curative for their clients. One could well be the helper's perceived ability to listen and wish to understand. Again, trainee therapists are often shown to do better with their clients than their experienced supervisors. Their enthusiasm and attentiveness are suggested as the curative factors.

It may be salutary to think to what extent the reader's Brief Gestalt Therapy is focused so that these curative conditions are in evidence. The method gives scope for all of them, as the following resume suggests:

The establishing of trust The dialogic attitude, the treatment of the client as an authority, are some of the common ways of describing Gestalt therapeutic mode. What they are meant to add up to is a therapeutic relationship that of itself may well be the major instrument of change and healing. The words 'emotionally charged and confiding relationship' are used. This phrase sits well with existential-phenomenological dialogue. In this the therapist reveals her sensate and emotional responses, as well as her imaginings and suggestions. She stays human, albeit in the context of and with awareness of the client as the major focus of attention.

A healing setting From their own therapy, readers are likely to recall the importance they may have given to factors in the setting of therapy. Regularity and predictability often have a special value. So do quiet, proper lighting and aesthetics, along with enough comfort in the sitting arrangements, and perhaps having materials such as paper and crayons and so forth available. These are not always on hand. They may be seen as what organisational theorists have called 'hygiene factors' (McGregor, 1960). Just as no one is likely to choose a job because the toilets are clean, so few people will choose a therapist because she has a nice view from her window. But sometimes people will leave jobs because the toilets are horrible. And they may languish in therapy where interruption is likely, or where the room is gloomy or cold. Gestalt attention to context, to background, argues for BGT therapists' focus on making the physical and emotional conditions of the work as enhancing as possible. The impact of the therapist's presence is nevertheless a good deal higher on this description of a healing setting than most other factors.

The arousal of hope There is an assumption in Gestalt that change is possible, indeed inevitable. People constantly reinvent themselves as they live each new day. The choice is between reinventing, and thus imitating the past, or inventing in the new context of the present. Some of the devices in BGT, such as the rating scales suggested later in this book, underline this assumption.

Encouraging changed behaviour outside the session This is a particular feature of BGT, where the small span of time available can often be made more fruitful by the invention by client and therapist of experiments that can be tried in the intervals between sessions.

Encouraging new ways of understanding oneself through corrective emotional experiences The underpinning of BGT, the dialogue, will for many people involve what this author terms a corrective emotional experience. It may even be the first time the client has had a sense of being attended to, listened to and valued for up to an hour at a time.

The phrase 'corrective emotional experience' has sometimes been applied to more questionable, even manipulative therapeutic intervention, such as the cultivation of transference neurosis. If it is removed from this miasma, and thought of straightforwardly, then it is arguable that some Gestalt methods, perhaps most famously the two-chair dialogue, are a route to catharsis. Since the time of Aristotle at least, this emotional purging has been recognised as freeing or enlightening. What may be less dramatic and at least as valuable in making the healing setting, is the relationship of listening, trust and openness that the Gestalt therapist aims for.

The high focus on immediate perception in BGT involves awareness of the emotion that accompanies all action. This again is in a sense corrective emotional experience. It is for many clients a revelation that they carry as much suppressed feeling as they do. That they have a degree of choice about their feelings is another likely satori, or awakening, in the work. 'Mini-satori' was a term coined by Perls. Its special relevance in BGT will be explained further in the next chapter.

A conceptual scheme or myth to explain symptoms It is salutary that the word 'myth' is used here. The Gestalt myth or hypothesis is that symptoms can be seen as evidence of blocks to healthy or fluent gestalt formation. The re-establishment of elastic or fluent gestalt formation is considered of itself to be the cure.

This myth does not preclude the content of other psychotherapeutic myths. Like the behaviourists, Gestalt practitioners assume that behaviour that has been learned can be unlearned or replaced with more functional behaviour. Like the analytic schools, they assume the multigenerational genesis of much unhappiness and dysfunction. In other words, the **process of gestalt formation** is the heart of the Gestalt therapeutic scheme, rather than the items of content which are at the centre of some others.

A ritual to help resolve symptoms The general openness about procedures in Gestalt Therapy means that clients can understand the wide variety of interventions that may be employed, within a clear framework. With dialogue as the underpinning experiment, other experiments will be devised as need arises and creativity suggests. They will be invented by either party, tried or discarded, and evaluated for their usefulness. This is the containing ritual of BGT.

These experiments may range through the immediate and the physical, such as standing in a new way, using muscular force, or breathing differently.

They may be in the sensate area, for example, in noticing internal sensing, or discovering how sensation from outside stimuli is habitually processed. They may be to do with emotion, and the ways it is blocked or released. They can be to do with memory, and the re-evocation of past scenes that still preoccupy the client. Or they may be to do with imagination, looking harder at fancied ambitions and hopes, fears or catastrophes, and rehearsing for the future. They may be to do with power, will, assertion, or whatever word is needed to describe volition and the lack of it as that affects the client. They are very often indeed to do with discovering and possibly changing the ways the client has of getting on with other people.

The group

There has been a waning of interest in many sorts of group therapy in recent years, as if the following prophecy has been forgotten:

> The probability that individual and long-range therapy might both be obsolete has not yet dawned on the vast majority of therapists and patients.... The individual session should be the exception rather than the rule. (Perls, 1992: xv)
>
> (Note: Individual in this context means with one person, rather than one-off.)

Group therapy is central to the training and practice of many Gestalt practitioners, so this topic will be covered in some depth in later chapters arranged as a separate section. These will contain suggestions of modifications which have been shown to maximise good outcomes for participants in 10-session groups in NHS and other settings.

It is difficult to understand why group therapy is not used more by the agencies that fund short-term work. Most of what brings people into therapy is to do with how they get on with themselves and other people. Each person's styles of relating are more likely to emerge, and have their impact reported, in a group, than with one other person. As will be reiterated in this book, group therapy is very often more effective for most participants than one-to-one therapy. It is also cheaper in terms of money and professional time.

Gestalt has much coherent theory of group therapy (e.g. Houston, 1998a, 1998b; Kepner, 1980). It is often an easy way of engaging clients and maintaining their engagement. Putting the discussion of it after that on individual work is by no means a way of indicating that it comes afterwards in value, in the opinion of this writer.

Experience as a river, not an iceberg

Gestalt psychotherapy requires a shift of perception from practitioners and clients alike. The shift is to noticing the present as the one reality where past and present meet, where whatever can be revealed will be revealed, and where change can happen. It is to noticing that the present, like a person, is an ever-fleeting time–space event made up of the subject and her world. This world is not primarily mind or soul or body or relationship or history or expectation, but all these among much else that come together in the consulting room as a dialogue.

Gestalt is concerned with dynamics, with flow. English is a wonderful language for describing the outer realities of the world, and this fluency can distort our sense of inner reality. Words like 'ego', 'id' and 'superego' can sound like things, parts of the mind, as a hand or mouth is part of the body. In Gestalt the Ego is seen as a way of doing rather than an entity; it is the function of managing contact with the environment, the available world.

The work of the Gestalt therapist is to keep the dialogue between the perceptual worlds of therapist and client in the foreground. The way the two interact, often termed the structure of the **contact between**, is seen as the major focus of diagnosis and treatment. These two, diagnosis and treatment, very often proceed together rather than sequentially. In the words of the first populariser of Gestalt Therapy, Fritz Perls: '… a combination, a synchronisation of analysis and reconditioning, is required' (1992: 215).

In a simple case, perhaps a recent bereavement, the patient might seek reassurance that he is not mad or ill. The therapist's task then may be simply to **be with** the anguished person for a few weeks, accepting his despair or catharsis, and an interventionist style might not be of use.

Many other people will arrive with any of a range of difficulties from physical symptoms through relational problems and substance abuse to problems with the social security (Tansella and Thornicroft, 1999). Where are the client and therapist to focus? One path with such people is to bring into focus the **foreground** problem, the one that is apparently the most distressing or preoccupying. Then there can be conversation about what change is hoped for in perception or behaviour, and range scales can with advantage be used to give an indication of how progress is to be monitored. An agreement is then sought, to focus awareness in that area. The therapist may even spell out her guess that what is being focused on will prove to be a fractal, a representation or analogue of other difficulties the patient is experiencing. So any learning about the particular may generalise to other areas of life.

Another Gestalt path might be to take the immediate process, for instance, a grasshoppering around and around from difficulty to difficulty as itself the focus for work. **Contact**, the way the client and therapist deal with each other in behaviour, content and feeling is the focus. The process is often described as **analysing the structure of the contact**. In this sense, BGT uses an examination of what goes on between client and therapist as the diagnostic as well as treatment method (Philippson, 1999). This book recognises the value of such immediacy. It also suggests other methods, including some apparently mechanistic aids, perhaps geared to therapists whose intuition is fallible (Melnick and Nevis, 1992).

Fritz Perls in his work, particularly in America, demonstrated ultra-brief therapy time and again. In his words: 'Most important of all, the achievement of a strong gestalt is itself the cure, for the figure of contact is not a sign of, but **is itself** the creative integration of experience' (Perls et al., 1951: 232).

This understanding is central to Gestalt, and may sit oddly with people trained in other psychotherapeutic disciplines. To have a good understanding of what is meant by achieving a strong gestalt, an outline of some of the central assumptions of Gestalt Therapy is needed. This is best reached by way of workshops and training. But for readers who are already generic therapists and who probably use some of the methods of Gestalt, a reminder is spelled out in the next chapter, on Theory.

The seminal text, *Gestalt Therapy* (Perls et al., 1951) has the subtitle, *Excitement and Growth in the Human Personality*. This points to the emphasis in Gestalt on enlivenment. This means rendering more alive, engaged, earnest when interested, playful and appropriately varied in response.

Another way of describing all this is in terms of Sartre's (1956) criteria of existentialism: **good faith and bad faith**. The words and actions that come from the heart, or the totality of a person, are said to be in good faith. Even the same actions, performed half-heartedly, with misgiving, indifferently, are in bad faith. They betray the psyche.

Attention to the nature of perception, and thus the nature of the behaviour of the person seeking therapy, is in the beginnings of Brief Gestalt Therapy. The aim of the work can be described as a move towards wholeheartedness or response in good faith, rather than only a narrow symptom reduction.

Summation

Brief Gestalt Therapy is for people; it does not set out to provide a formulaic treatment for cases or examples of categories of mental distress. Instead, based on well-tried practices of Gestalt Therapy, it requires both therapist and client to work urgently and truthfully on the dominant issues which present themselves here and now. People are not to be bent to the shape of the treatment, but rather the other way about. That is a challenge to the therapist, who needs to find ways of increasing her spontaneity and appropriate inventiveness of response to each unique scene and person. This book seeks to show the therapist ways of meeting this exciting challenge.

2

The Gestalt Approach: Theory Related to Brief Intervention

> Those who are enamoured of practice without science are like the pilot who gets into a ship without rudder or compass and who never has any certainty where he is going. (Leonardo da Vinci, 1952, G 8r)

For readers who come from other disciplines, here is a short outline of some elements of this approach, and its historical context.

> Gestalt Therapy, like many theories of change and theories of psychotherapy, was born of disquiet, excitement and consequent creative thinking. Like all psychotherapeutic theories, it is a set of hypotheses to describe reality and indicate a coherent system of therapeutic assumptions and methods. It does not stem from scientific certainty, but is the best the inventors can manage with the data they possess.

Just as the psychoanalytic theories have evolved and been the subject of much internal dispute since the time of Freud, in something of the same way, different emphases are evident in Gestalt theory. Frederick, generally known as Fritz, Perls, the best-known early writer on Gestalt Therapy, trained and worked as a psychoanalyst. He was steeped in the psychoanalytic theories, which had first been brought into being fifty years before by the disquiet, excitement and consequent creative thinking of Sigmund Freud. But it was by no means only Freud who influenced him.

Kurt Goldstein, the neurologist who worked on the differentiation between right and left hemispheres of the brain, and on holism in its many aspects, was an early influence on Perls and his theory. Other strong influences in Gestalt Therapy include Moreno's (1946) social experimentation; a version of existentialism; Kurt Lewin's field theory; a kind of phenomenology; and some Zen concepts. Perls was directly influenced by Karen Horney and Wilhelm Reich, before the latter also broke away from psychoanalysis. Psychoanalytic assumptions are either continued in Gestalt, or directly challenged in the theory. In other words, psychoanalysis is continually honoured either in the breach or the observance. Perls's early work, *Ego, Hunger and Aggression* (1947), was sub-titled *A Revision of Freud's Theory and Method.*

The development of Gestalt Therapy

Perls came to question some of the assumptions and most of the methodology of psychoanalysis. He became sceptical of whether the aetiology of the neuroses was inevitably sexual. He became convinced of the analogy between styles of eating and of taking in, assimilating or rejecting of all experience.

He perceived the value of what is now called intersubjectivity, the dialogue between therapist and client, rather than the more passive and abstinent style of the analyst. He became fascinated with the truly immediate, and so brought into being a therapeutic theory of the process of perception and interaction with the world. This was strongly influenced by Kurt Goldstein (1939), the neurologist already mentioned, and Kurt Lewin (1951), a social psychologist, to whom the field theory that is central to Gestalt Therapy is attributable.

Perls believed that perception is not atomistic, but is organised by the mind into fields; in other words it is to do with **gestalt formation** and is holistic, as was described in the last chapter. (This led to the use of the word Gestalt, with a capital G, as the name of the therapy itself.) His exposure to Goldstein and Lewin contributed to this major departure from much psychoanalytic theory. As well as the neuroses, the major pathologies can be described in field theory terms (Maibaum, 1992). So it seems appropriate to begin by making another attempt to make clear the meaning of this phrase, 'gestalt formation'.

A gestalt is an organised field of data. The foreground of this will be to do with the dominant **need**, the next item with which the **organism**, the totality of the person concerned, is dealing. Perls suggests that most of what we do is in response to a hierarchy of need or want (Maslow, 1956). In health, the organism presents to awareness the next need, which is then fulfilled, thus losing interest and making room for another need to emerge through a new gestalt formation. These needs are not just a simple response only to drives or other internal dynamics. A gestalt is an organised field of perception, which probably includes bits of the subject's history and aspirations, as well as present circumstances, set habits, and all else that is operant at that moment. Gestalt formation is in other words an organisation of a field, relating to the past, the future and the environment, to the internal and the external world.

Perls describes a cycle of what he calls the interdependency of **organism**, the subject or protagonist, and **environment**, by which he meant whatever in the outside world had present significance:

1. The disturbing factor, which may be:
   (a) An external disturber – a demand put upon us, or any interference that puts us on the defensive;
   (b) An internal disturbance – a need which has gathered enough momentum to strive for gratification and which requires:
2. The creation of an image or reality (plus–minus function and figure–background phenomena);
3. The answer to the situation aiming at:
4. A decrease of tension – achievement of gratification or compliance with the demands resulting in:
5. The return of the organism to balance. (Perls, 1992: 43)

This cycle was adapted to diagrammatic form by Zinker (1977). Joseph Zinker elaborated this Gestalt model, into the Cycle of Experience or Awareness. It suggests that all experience starts with some **sensory impact** from within or without. This mounts in intensity until it enters **awareness**. Then it leads to greater excitation, **emotionality**, and the **search** for solutions or plans of **action**. Milliseconds, rather than the time it takes to write or read these lines, may be all that are required for these stages to occur. Next, if all goes well, some action or **contact** in the world, is undertaken. Last, there is some assimilative or learning process, which will lead to quiescence and sense of **completion**, or else to a new cycle of experience.

A strong gestalt is one that happens with life and clarity and without interruption. A simple example perhaps might be a warm greeting at an unexpected meeting. If recognition is followed by feelings of affection and these communicate as a happy shout or wave or hug, the wholeheartedness of the episode will be apparent.

But blocking, interruption or cutting off can occur between any of the stages just described. At another unexpected meeting someone may register that he does not want to be seen with his companion in these circumstances. He may recall an unpaid debt between him and the person just recognised. He may feel irritated that this other person is appearing at the same prestigious event to which he felt honoured to be invited. In strong gestalt formation, he will know just what he wants to do about this, whether in deliberate avoidance or frank confession or whatever. If he experiences more conflict, a gestalt will not form readily. He may even fail to recognise this other person who represents a bluebottle in the ointment of his evening out. The likelihood is that, if not blankness, a certain lacklustre or fumbling quality will be in his greeting and meeting.

In a simple example, Tommy is walking down the street, walking almost on air, as he has just heard that he has passed his exam, and has had a small win on the lottery. He sees Jenny (an external disturbing factor, 1(a)) and grins and waves to her. She notices, but turns away and goes into a shop. Jenny owes him money and feels deeply unwilling to face him, as they have recently had a row on the subject. But Tommy's circumstances, and so his perceptual field, have shifted since the row. He notices how pretty she is, how unimportant money seems to him at this moment (2), and how much he wants her to go out with him on Saturday. He pursues her into the shop (3). In this example, (4) and (5) are not described. For Tommy, arranging to take Jenny out might fulfil (4) the contact stage of this gestalt, and free him (5) to focus on his own shopping or whatever.

Different psychologies describe events in different ways. Gestalt Therapy emphasises the way the field of perception is organised, and seeks to develop more **awareness** in gestalt formation, livelier **contact** between subject and environment, whether that environment is human or other, and appropriate **flexibility of response**.

From the vignette here, we do not know whether Tommy is disconcertingly impulsive, leaping from money lending to blame to apparent forgiveness in a way that creates distrust in others and perhaps himself. We do not know whether Jenny is responding to something like that perception of him as she scuttles off, or whether she is someone who is habitually avoidant, or is quite other.

An isolated incident like this is in Gestalt the starting place for finding the meaning given to it by the protagonist. The therapist does not assume that any behaviour has a universal or common meaning. The phenomenological method, of creating space for noticing more and more of the background at any moment, is the bedrock of the method.

So, should these descriptions fit, Tommy might be interested in steadying the impulsiveness of his gestalt formation and response. Jenny might, on the other hand, want to achieve more flexibility of response. The therapist would seek to raise awareness of Tommy's or Jenny's process of gestalt formation. A great deal of attention would be given to what went on between therapist and client, as it occurred in the therapy room, rather than just to what was reported from elsewhere.

They would, for example, look for whether what either of them, therapist or client, did, was concerned with oughts and musts from introjected commands, and how much they were behaving in response to what Perls calls the **wisdom of the organism**. This is the ability he sees us all having, to sort, from the myriad possibilities, and probably at immense speed, that action, that decision, which best serves in this place at this time for this person. He thus postulates the organism as, along with all its other functions, an unconscious sorting house. This sorting and prioritising happens at an unaware level. It is helped to good functioning, however, by raising awareness of the way each of us makes our own private sense of our world and its events.

The unaware or unconscious

In health, many functions of the organism, mercifully, are out of awareness. Digestion, assimilation, much self-reparation, and that prioritisation of need that results in awareness, are a few such processes. It is sometimes assumed that Gestalt denies the existence of unconscious processes (Whines, 1999). Though that is not true, it is true that Gestalt theorists believe that concentrating on **aware** processes will be enough to deconstruct blocks to fluent gestalt formation.

Zen philosophers advise that we cultivate the top three inches. By dealing with the obvious, the manifestation here in the room, rather than theorising to the patient about possible unconscious connections or sources of what is showing here, Gestalt therapists stay with what is verifiable.

> I believe that this is the great thing to understand: *that awareness per se – by and of itself – can be curative*. Because with full awareness you become aware of this organismic self-regulation, you can let the organism take over without interfering, without interrupting; we can rely on the wisdom of the organism. And the contrast to this is the whole pathology of self-manipulation, environmental control and so on, that interferes with this subtle organismic self-control. (Perls, 1969: 37)

Theory and jargon

Jargon, professional insider language, can be an immensely useful shorthand at times. It can also mystify. One reason for this is that one term is sometimes used with more than one meaning. Elsewhere (Houston, 1993: 207), I have pointed out the different meanings given, for example, to the term projective identification. Inclusion, as another example, is used in Gestalt with a quite different meaning from that given to it by Schutz (1966).

Calling a spade a spade sounds a safe occupation. When the word is used to mean both spade and wheelbarrow, confusion will result, even though two speakers know that they are talking about gardening, and make their parallel senses of each other's statements. I have witnessed something of the same kind happening between psychotherapists, often enough to make me labour this point.

However, in this chapter on theory I shall name a number of Gestalt concepts that are as relevant in BGT as in longer work, and give some brief explanation of them.

Confrontation

In many psychotherapies nowadays, and certainly in Gestalt, there is emphasis on **being with** rather than **doing to** the client. Confrontation is seen as suspect. Looking at the general theory of Gestalt Therapy as we adapt it or ourselves to brief interventions, it seems important to allow a short digression on this notion of confrontation.

At heart the word suggests facing, or coming face to face with. Arguably this is central to much good therapy. Until someone comes face to face with, or is really aware of, his perceptions and behaviour, he lacks a sense of what he needs or how to achieve it. BGT, or any therapy, often needs in this particular sense to be confrontational, if the time available is to be best used. Gestalt suggests that people benefit from being confronted with the obvious, with their own reality as revealed to the therapist. This may at times be uncomfortable, as suddenly seeing one's face in a mirror can be. It is still very different from being challenged to change or confronted with some demand from the therapist.

Organism

'Organism' is Perls's word to describe the whole being. This is a central integrative concept in Gestalt Therapy, and will be referred to many times in this book. It often overlaps with the concepts **subject** or **protagonist**, as they are used in other theories. The difference is that in Gestalt it serves both to differentiate from the environment, and to stress that organism and environment are indivisible. This seemingly complicated idea is not unique to Gestalt Therapy. Winnicott (1959: 99) in a famous quotation exemplifies the same idea: 'There is no such thing as a baby … if you show me a baby, you certainly show me also someone caring for the baby, or at least a pram with someone's eyes glued to it'. Stern's (1985) theory too supports the Gestalt belief in organismic integrity. What is meant by this is the holistic nature of humans. Mind, body and spirit do not need to be separated as concepts in Gestalt, since these aspects of life operate as a unity. There is always an integrity, in the sense of co-operation or some other interaction between the sensoric, motoric and cognitive aspects of a person.

In support of this holistic view, BGT therapeutic methods similarly address many aspects of living besides the verbal. Current research supports this emphasis (Kolk et al., 1996). Post-traumatic stress disorder researchers, for example, suggest that trauma has a strong impact on right hemispheric functioning, and is more responsive to non-verbal than verbal intervention. Avery (1999) quotes this '"physio-neurosis of trauma" as changing a person's ability to widen the perceptual field, so that they have a narrowing of attention which does not allow other aspects of their life to become figural'. (p. 55) In Gestalt theory, they have formed **fixed gestalts**. The need to surprise, to look afresh, to reverse, and play in many ways besides the verbal, with such fixed perceptions, is demonstrated at length in the Hefferline section of Perls et al. (1951).

Contact

Contact, another central interest in Gestalt Therapy, again gives rise to intervention at more than just the verbal level.

> Let us understand contacting, awareness and motor response in the broadest sense, to include appetite and rejection, approaching and avoiding, sensing, feeling, manipulating, estimating, communicating, fighting etc – every kind of living relation that occurs at the boundary in the interaction of the organism and environment. (Perls et al., 1951: 229)

Contact in this sense takes in both the intersubjective, Buber's (1970) I–Thou, and all the other objects of what in Gestalt is termed **aggression**. The term is used here in its root Latin sense of action, reaching out, handling, dealing with, as well as the list of behaviours in the quotation above. It can be roughly summed up as **outwardly-directed activity**.

Fritz Perls extended the psychoanalytic attention to *hic et nunc*, the here and now, so the Gestalt therapist focuses heavily on what is termed the **contact boundary**. This mysterious and probably unnecessary phrase can be rendered as what happens to each party when people meet. Alongside and sometimes in spite of what may be said, there is constant, richly informative play of approach and retreat, of fear or warmth or other feeling, of changing pace, mirroring, and much else. This process was commented on to enormous effect in the early days of Gestalt Therapy by Laura Perls.

Dialogue

Laura Perls, the wife of Fritz, is less well known than he was. Yet she appears to have been the first and major influence in making Gestalt therapeutic relationship **dialogic**. In its roots this word means simply talking over thoroughly, or talking through. Here it is used to mean talking not just about psychotherapeutic theories, but rather attempting to convey the immediate reality of what is going on between therapist and client, or between group members, and them and the therapist. It is staying in the present, staying now.

> This ephemeral moment, this now, does not land from nowhere, like a butterfly fluttering heedless on the summer air. It results from the totality of that person at that instant. It comes from the accumulation of gene history, race history, acculturation, personal history and circumstance, and what that person has learned, or made of, a million other moments.

Laura Perls's style was quietly warm and listening, and acceptant of the world of the other, in marked contrast to her husband's more flamboyant and confrontational manner. Other early Gestalt practitioners emphasised this inclusive style, demonstrated to such memorable effect by Laura Perls. Part of that early theory of contact is preserved and has been developed theoretically in attention not just to moments of contact, but to 'tight sequencing' (Polster, 1991).

Contact, then, is the process by which both therapist and the person or people in therapy deal with each other. This is seen as the co-creation of a **between**, a possibly ever-changing set of responses influenced by and influencing each party to it (Buber, 1970). The central importance in humans of this dialogue or interaction is suggested not only by Fairbairn (1952), Sullivan (1954) and other theorists, but in developmental theory. Stern's (1985) observations of infant behaviour have led to his claim that the development of personality begins from birth onwards in the interactions of the child with its carers.

Deconstruction

The slogan **separate to integrate** is used to describe Gestalt Therapy's emphasis on **deconstruction**, the analysis of unwieldy integrations or of the sense of fragmentation. This comes before new integration. The section on the Gestalt theory of change adds to this description.

Zones of awareness

Perls described three zones: (a) Internal world; (b) Outer world; (c) Maja.

The **internal world** is, in his terms, the organism working for its own preservation and evolution, or working towards health.

The **external world** is just that, the actuality of that which is outside.

The **maja** is the fantasy inside each person. It is the capacity to fantasise and rehearse and imagine. It is also the web of old messages, fears, beliefs and more, which tends to get in the way of easy gestalt formation and full contact. It corresponds in many ways, though not altogether, to Stern's concept of The Narrative Self.

The mechanisms which form or maintain maja, and thus influence people's style of contact, are: (a) Introjection; (b) Deflection; (c) Retroflection; (d) Projection.

Introjection is likened to the swallowing whole of the unchewed. Beliefs and attitudes acquired from parents or other influential figures, especially in early life, are often introjects. Many of these are useful or even necessary shorthand. For an experienced driver, the muscles seem to know how to drive a car, and a verbal description might prove hard. Driving technique is largely introjected rather than assimilated. It then translates to a repertoire of behaviours that move the driver about the country and still leave her free for much of the time, to look at the landscape or listen to the radio.

In the same way, many social norms are taken on board without questioning, and lead to socially-appropriate responses. This is fine if the norms are to do with the hygienic evacuation of bodily waste, say. But many other beliefs and practices may be introjected, and held as part of the maja, with more distressing results. Beliefs that sex is wicked or that a neighbouring ethnic group is stupid or evil are among many common introjects that can lead to psychological pain or even to war.

Confluence, the merging of self and other, or of organism and environment, is a Gestalt concept which is related to introjection. Like all these notions, it can be seen as sometimes desirable, as in orgasm, or undesirable, if it means a constant yielding to the needs of dominant others (Polster, 1993).

Deflection is the turning aside rather than letting in of data, stimuli or even feelings. Most people are adept at this. The wily child reminded of bedtime at once begins some homework or piano practice. The bereaved husband throws himself into his work or hobby. The woman who is asked an uncomfortable question changes the subject by asking where her questioner bought her beautiful shoes.

Retroflection is turning back on oneself. It is making oneself the object as well as the subject. A young woman strokes her own hair. Perhaps this is a substitute for that attention from the inarticulate young man beside her. Perhaps she strokes her own hair because she is too embarrassed to express her true need, which is to stroke his. In either case, subject and object have been made one. This concept is particular to Gestalt, and has over the years come to include what in other psychologies would be called inhibition and repression. It is now sometimes used to describe the opposite of being expressive (Parlett and Hemming, 1996).

Projection is literally a throwing forward. It is the attributing to another what belongs to oneself. Perls calls it a screen phenomenon, likening it to a cinema projector. In the same way, he suggests that the person who behaves as if the therapist is his parent or some other person, is projecting.

> Special attention should be shown to the process of projection, which in itself is not a transference, but a 'screen' phenomenon. The film of a motion picture is not taken out of the projector and transferred on to the screen but remains in the machine and is merely projected. (Perls, 1992: 288)

In recent times transference and counter-transference have entered the vocabulary and understanding of Gestalt therapists. It is interesting, especially in thinking about brief therapy, to note that the ex-psychoanalyst Perls gave short shrift to this idea which remains so central in some schools.

> In other words, dealing with the transference means an unnecessary complication – a waste of time. If I can draw water from the tap in my room, it is unnecessary to go down to the well. (Perls, 1992: 290)

It is arguable that the Gestalt concepts of projection, introjection and retroflection allow a precise and sufficient description of the phenomena of transference and counter-transference, and that these latter terms are more a fashion item than a useful addition to the theory.

On the other side it can be argued that transference is not only a useful concept, but one so prevalent in psychotherapy, that it is a little prissy to avoid it. It is perhaps worth noting, however, that many students use the concepts in very narrow ways. Transference is often used only to describe parental transference, rather than in the more informative general way well demonstrated by Casement (1985). Counter-transference, conversely, has in general usage sagged into meaning whatever emotions the therapist feels towards the client. These distortions can be taken as another argument for avoiding jargon wherever possible.

Resistance as assistance

Perls moves beyond psychoanalytic theory again in his insistence that resistances, defences, need to be understood as the client's assistances. He sees them as idiosyncratic inventions, lighted on at some time of threat. Illuminating their presence, structure and function in the therapy room is part of the deconstructive work mentioned above. The resulting changed awareness is seen as the necessary condition for change to take place. And it is change in itself.

Theory of change

Change is often assumed in Gestalt Therapy to happen in a way that is termed paradoxical. This implies that it comes about as a result of full acceptance of what is, rather than a striving to be different (Beisser, 1970). The paradoxical theory of change, though dear to Gestalt practitioners, is not unique to that therapy. Carl Rogers's unconfrontational style, for example, has the same implicit assumption. Brian Thorne (1999), a person-centred practitioner, describes this kind of change, as well as supporting the possible efficacy of brief work:

> The notion that meaningful change can only come about as the result of long and painstaking processes is clearly untrue. What is more, profound and instant change more often than not comes as the result of a highly charged encounter with another person or with a perception of reality which drives away fear. (p. 7)

This vivid description may be said to coincide with what Gestalt terms 'paradoxical' change. The 'highly-charged encounter' in therapy is almost always, in my experience, to do with finally allowing into awareness, into the witnessed present, powerful love or fear that has for long been kept at bay.

Transformative experience

Perls wrote sternly against the idea of the instant turn-on, of the kind often sought in groups at the time he was writing. But he often used the term mini-satori to describe the jolt, the change of perception, that is in line with the 'excitement and growth in the human personality' in the title of his major work. What he was talking about is the arguably necessary shift from a habitual perceptive stance, to one that is new, has more awareness, and is in the interests of the perceiver.

In another setting, the feminists coined the word 'click', to describe a similar moment, when women who might have all the intellectual understanding of the feminist position, of social oppression of women and so forth, suddenly lurch into an emotional realisation. One woman describes how seeing her husband step over the washing on the stairs gave her this instant awakening to the huge role differences she had fostered or accepted in her own life, and a consequent freedom to change.

Such experiences may or may not happen in good therapy. They are not mandatory. They are very valuable. For many people they are to be remembered gratefully and with wonder for the rest of life if they do occur, in or out of a formal setting. In brief therapy, my experience is that such useful small miracles are more likely if the possibility of them is near the therapist's awareness. Her nose for anthenticity is very important here. Positive transference can bring about something of the same sense of a changed world. Until it is understood for what it is, and translated back to its true place in the client's life, it is no more than the instant turn-on Perls decried.

Other routes to change are implicit in Gestalt. One could be called Aristotelian or mimetic learning, through exposure to the non-judgemental dialogic presence of the therapist. Another is through the creativity of experimenting with behaviours or contexts that are novel. Much of the first, later called the second, volume of Gestalt Therapy (Perls et al., 1951) was a series of experiments designed to jolt the subject out of habits of perception. The overall aim of such work is to do with giving fresh value, newness and flexibility of response. This arguably involves change, but it is not paradoxical change in the technical meaning of the phrase. So the reality of the Gestalt theory of change in practice is that it is more various than is sometimes acknowledged. It is in line with more than one developmental theory, as people themselves seem to be.

Theory of people

The theory of people in Gestalt is holistic, emphasising the indivisibility of organism and environment. It is optimistic, assuming tendency or capacity for growth and excitement, in the words of the subtitle of the major theory book, **excitement and growth in the human personality** (Perls et al., 1951). Daniel Stern's (1985) theory of development expresses the Gestalt interest in both intersubjectivity, and the laying down of benign and other fixed gestalts or what Stern calls Repeated Interactions that are Generalised, or RIGs, in early and indeed later life. Gestalt emphasises the tendency in the human mind towards integration, organisation, co-operation. However, **indivisibility of organism and**

environment is a central concept in Gestalt, with all that implies about mutual influence, and about limitation. Perception, as has already been said, is seen as occurring within a field. **Need** is the organiser of that field.

Summation

BGT theory can be seen as a river, ever-changing and yet clearly bounded. The constants helping form these theoretical boundaries or banks are:

1. A dialogic attitude in the therapist;
2. Full attention to the present;
3. Constant relation of what is figural to its context.

Even the banks, however, will modify over time.

Gestalt practitioners pay attention to the holism, the indivisible nature of person and world, of organism and environment.

They assume that patterns of perception, behaviour and interaction will be demonstrated by the client in the here and now, and can be treated at ego level.

This holistic view extends in BGT to an integration by the therapist of insights and methods from other schools of therapy, where these seem likely to be of use to the client. Laura Perls's dictum that **each new client needs a new therapy** is seen to be of particular value in brief work.

Although insight about the assumed causes of distress often occurs, it is not a primary focus of BGT. It is often assumed in other schools that depth of therapy can only be achieved by a thorough exploration of the past. BGT assumes rather that the primary aim must be to deal fully, perceptively and confrontationally with what manifests in the present.

Practice points

In brief work with most clients, the principles of general Gestalt Therapy theory obtain. Any differences are differences of emphasis. The elements of Gestalt theory that can usefully be stressed in BGT include:

High awareness of **context**, as much as can possibly be discovered about the world the client makes or sees, and which has an internal logical connection to the distress she experiences.

Focused awareness on what seems to be the dominant need, with the assumption that this may well be a fractal of the whole. Attention to one locus of distress may well reduce other distress too or lead to more general wellbeing.

Spontaneity and creativity in the therapist, to optimise the heightening of awareness.

Attunement to the client, and comment on the nature of the contact.

Recognition that overextensive attention to history is seldom appropriate within the short time available.

Among the likely differences from longer-term therapy are:

The devising and monitoring of experiments to be done between sessions. These are more in line with one volume of Gestalt Therapy (Perls et al., 1951) than with much modern practice.

Therapist willingness to be proactive if need be, in holding to the agreed focus or foci. Longer-term work is likely to be more client-led.

Heightened attention to **time**.

The shared assumption that the episode of therapy might constitute only **one stage** of new learning.

3

The Assessment

Ask advice of him who governs himself well. (Leonardo da Vinci, 1952: H 118 v)

The word assessment has a somewhat cold ring. Yet it is to do with some of the most valuable aspects of BGT, and it is always a strand of the work of BGT from beginning to end. It includes the recognition of patterns, of styles of contact, of signs, as well as the symptoms the client reports. A large concentration on assessment is likely at the beginning, in many episodes of therapy. '… Any therapeutic intervention in a therapist's office, we think, is preceded by more or less conscious diagnostic evaluations' (Fuhr et al., 2000). That is the rationale for placing this chapter where it is. It is part of the beginning, certainly. And it may be the whole work of some episodes of BGT.

> Noting what the client seems to need, noting what interventions seem to work and what others do not, noting the minutiae of interaction, and modifying therapist behaviour in the light of all this, is the continuous assessment process that will be evinced in fluid gestalt formation.

At the same time, the client is inevitably making his own judgements as he goes along, and modifying what he does, believes and expects in the light of them. When this process is encouraged into awareness and becomes shared, it will be much of the gold of the dialogue in the therapy room.

Frank (1973) suggests that the common task of all therapy is the restoration of morale. An aspect of this restoration is to accord dignity and worth to the distressed person. One way in which BGT seeks to do this is by stressing the mutuality there is in assessment as well as other aspects of therapy. It is important that the therapist uses observation and judgement. It is as vital that the client too is offered scope for questioning, testing, judging and problem-solving. This mutuality is the beginning of therapeutic dialogue.

In some instances BGT in its entirety can usefully be seen simply as an assessment process. There are people who risk falling through the cracks of the system in which they appear, and are sent to a therapist rather more for the sake of the system than primarily for their own good. These include misfits in workplaces; patients who are unresponsive to repeated medical treatment; people who cannot be understood because of difference across a wide spectrum from culture to disability to language, and much more.

With such people, the sociological aspects of their difficulties may merit at least six or eight therapeutic encounters devoted to naming as clearly as may be what their difficulties are, and working out with them what next steps they want to take after seeing the therapist.

The first meeting

The therapeutic system, group or pair, has begun to emerge before this first face to face moment. Perhaps like a foetus *in utero*, this system will already have created some characteristics in these pre-contact times. In the few weeks usually allotted to brief therapy, it is wasteful to have to devote unnecessary time to deconstructing impressions and prejudices about therapy and the therapist. I use the word unnecessary. Some such work is likely to be the necessary central task with certain people, for instance those who are habitually scared and untrusting.

What is unnecessary is to have most people arrive in the consulting room having been told by a doctor that, for example, they are very unlikely to benefit, but might as well try talking to the therapist. Others may regularly arrive from a different source having heard that the therapist is a wonder worker who will have them sorted in no time. Both these pre-contact statements are direct quotations from referral sources. The reader will perhaps know many such examples. With this warning, and a reminder to act on the suggestions in Chapter 4, this chapter focuses on the tasks of therapist and client that go alongside and are woven into their first contact.

Informing

Contact, in the Gestalt sense of interaction of all kinds, is generally the main instrument of healing and change. But therapeutic contact is purposeful. Beginning therapists are sometimes carried away by the notion of tracking, of following and commenting, rather than leading. BGT is best carried out with a skilled mixture of these two, plus patient informing. So BGT assessment includes or begins with as clear statements as can be managed about what the therapist can offer. As an example, here is a portmanteau version of such an introduction in one-to-one work. Having heard what the client wants to say, the therapist is likely before the end of the first session to have come back with responses that will not be delivered in one fell swoop as quoted here, but will add up to something along these lines:

> The way this agency works, I can offer you up to eight 50-minute sessions at this time each week, this counting as the first one. My hope is that we can talk together in that time to bring more into awareness what is going on for you at the moment. It can be too easy to stay with words and lose a sense of all else. So what I've often found of use to people is to vary talking with drawing or movement or any other experiment that looks as if it might help you get clearer, or work something out in some way.
>
> You'll see that I am interested in everything about you that may shed light on your difficulties, and on how you can cope better. For instance, I've just noticed that I'm breathing somewhere in my throat at the moment, and my heart's beating fast. I'm not sure if it's just that I'm nervous at meeting you for the first time. Oh, I see now that you're sitting very still. Maybe we're both not breathing much. I suppose we could stop breathing altogether. What do you suggest?
>
> [The meaning of the stopped breath is explored briefly, and the therapist suggests that they monitor each other and comment if the other person seems to breathe shallowly again.]
>
> It's likely that you will think of useful experiments to do, once you get the hang of this way of working. In other words, I am not setting myself up to know your answers. I shall work away to raise your awareness, along with mine. The hope is that through these meetings you can be back in what feels to you the right sort of flow in your life, as you've described that to me. At the least, we shall get to know more about how you get upset, how you block yourself from thinking about consequences, and how at other times you manage not to get into that problem.

This greatly abbreviated and condensed extract from an assessment meeting shows the BGT stress on demonstrating the sharing of power with the client, as early as possible. It also shows the therapist's willingness to reveal her present experience in a phenomenological exploration, where she thinks that will be useful to the client.

The client here was a convicted offender whose low violence threshold was his reason for seeking therapy via his doctor. He was not especially articulate or psychologically sophisticated in an academic way, and the therapist's choice of words takes account of this. (His psychological sophistication in terms of being street-wise was immense. It had been his survival mechanism since his childhood in a family where both parents reportedly drank to excess.)

The example here is from one-to-one therapy. As clear an exposition is needed at the beginning of a BGT group.

Another aspect of the assessment session shown here is that the therapist offers an example of how she will work. This is much as an analyst might offer a trial interpretation in a first session of brief therapy. The intention in BGT assessment is in part to offer a taste of what is to come, so that the client has more data on which to base a decision about whether to continue. Such a speedy introduction of Gestalt methods has been used successfully with many BGT clients. But there are others who seem nervous, suspicious, ill-at-ease or give other clear indications that they are likely to respond better to a slower, or perhaps a less invasive, observation at the beginning. That said, people are built to last.

> By and large, we are often less frail than some psychotherapeutic approaches assume. Friendly directness, founded on honest interest rather than the desire to display therapeutic expertise, is generally a sound way of working that will allow ease and latitude to both people in individual therapy, or to the whole group if that is the setting.

As in an assessment session, you the reader have now been given a taste of BGT, of the process of therapy. Now we return to content, to what is there for the therapist and the client in turn to consider before agreeing to work together.

Which clients are suitable for Brief Gestalt Therapy?

Psychologically-minded people with a capacity for maintaining relationships are likely to do well in brief or any other form of therapy. Therapists who are primarily interested in getting impressive results in outcome research are likely to take to heart these criteria, when choosing whom to treat.

In reality, many people who are offered the opportunity of brief therapy may not have these optimistic traits. These clients have probably arrived at the surgery with physical symptoms, expecting perhaps to have medicine by way of treatment.

Workplace counselling is another arena of very brief intervention. At times a distressed employee may have wanted time off for emotional disturbance or headaches or whatever, and may have huge ambivalence about being offered, or as he sees it, being sent for, counselling.

There are many lists of what makes for suitability or otherwise (Burton, 1998: 95–6), and they make helpful guides or warnings, but most of these are concerned with facets of mental health. BGT is concerned with the whole person, and more than that, the field operant at the time of referral.

The cautious view is offered here, that the right partnership is that of a willing therapist with a willing client.

This statement may at first appear somewhat feckless or naive. For example, the reader may well reflect that in some ways many or most patients are likely to be in part unwilling, conflicted about a talking treatment, particularly in the United Kingdom. There are also patients who are very willing, but about whom the therapist may feel reluctant.

This is a two-sided decision. The phenomenological responses of the therapist need to be respected by her. She needs to know herself and her capacities pretty well, to achieve an informed willingness or reluctance to work with someone. She needs insightful and intelligent supervision. She also needs to be able to judge rather quickly whether she has the sense that she can be, or at least wants to be, of use to the patient within the limits of the time available. In practice this may often mean that she follows some of Malan's (1982: 104) rejection criteria: 'history of serious suicide attempts; drug addiction; long-term hospitalisation; more than one episode of ECT; chronic alcoholism; incapacitating chronic obsessional symptoms; gross destructive or self-destructive acting-out'. But she remains open to the person as well as the description, and so may take on some people for whom there might be, on paper, a poor prediction of successful outcome. In other words, BGT is not a beginner's task.

Most of us can recall patients for whom there were many contra-indications for Brief Therapy in the literature, but who have nevertheless made good or very good use of the opportunity (Burton, 1998). Likewise there are others who read on paper like suitable candidates, but who do not thrive, from some cause not spotted straightaway by the therapist, but possibly relating to her.

> A robust referral system is intrinsic to the work, and in Primary Care or Workplace Counselling, Gestalt therapists are well advised to offer seminars where referral criteria and methodology, including clarity about the extent and limits of confidentiality, can be agreed with all the people involved. This is an aspect of the holistic view encouraged in this approach.

This is a crucial example of attention to the background as well as the foreground of therapy. Where there is ease, trust and frequent contact between the therapist, other professionals and any administrators who are involved in appointment-making and so forth, the therapy itself is likely to be affected for the better. Aggressing this aspect of the work, in the Gestalt sense of taking positive action to set up favourable conditions, is part of the therapist's task.

Some people arrive for therapy less because they seek it, than because other people do not know what to do with them. There are two warnings to reiterate about such occasions. The first is a reminder to make clear to whoever does the referring that you are a therapist, not a befriender or social worker. Alongside this is the truth that in a poorly-run workplace or other system, there may be psychological casualties: if the therapist does not attend to them, they may be dismissed or go mad. So purism needs to be tempered with pragmatism, or charity.

The other warning is about accepting clients whose culture and ethnicity is a complete mystery to the therapist. A supervisee was puzzled that a Thai client failed to come back after two sessions. According to him, he had seemed very pleased with the first meeting, and very smiling and cheerful. However, the therapist had been urging cathartic responses, unaware of the Thai concept of 'cool heart', which dictates that any display of uncomfortable emotion, or confrontational behaviour, is unacceptable.

Another supervisee complained how giggly she found a Japanese client. She had not understood that Japanese giggling is very often a show of extreme embarrassment, rather than mirth. Nor had she taken on board that it is not socially acceptable to Japanese people to ask them questions to which they do not know the answer.

These are two tiny examples of the chasm of failed communication there can be between the cultural assumptions of the therapist, and those of the people she is with. Awareness of such potential difficulties needs to be there as the therapist decides if she is willing or not to work with a particular person. Willingness, in this context, does not mean impetuosity or denial of the field on the part of the therapist.

Fore-contact

What happens before therapist and client meet may have a profound effect on their whole work together. A famous slogan from Chaos Theory is that 'there is sensitive dependence on initial conditions in non-linear systems' (Gleick, 1988). Therapeutic encounters are ephemeral, but may turn out to be most potently influential non-linear systems.

In training, practitioners have learnt to be sensitive to nuances of what people do in entering, in greeting, in how they choose a seat and sit, and so forth. They have probably also learned not to be over-confident of all these first impressions. **Intuition scores some bull's eyes, and at least an equal number of wides**.

The client is usually working away as sensitively as the therapist, noticing what the therapist does and omits; the difference is that she may not have learned to let data lie around on the desktop of her mind before filing it. The therapist who is unwittingly showing in her lacklustre eye the signs of last night's party, or who has attempted to stuff a nasty phone call out of awareness, may, without wanting to, give a prospective client some alarming data. The evidence is that once there is some bond, some shared experience, then a pale face or a mishearing or other error is likely to be far more tolerable to the client. He has good experience to set alongside a moment's bad experience of the therapist.

I have laboured this point, because I see it as massively important in brief therapy, where it may be wasteful of the client's or group's time to spend some of the therapy on iatrogenic issues. This medical word means originating in the doctor. It is a word to keep therapists humble. Certainly there are people who come to brief therapy who have trouble trusting people, and that may show from the start, and may be the primary focus of the work. What is talked of here is an unhelpful imposition of the therapist's way of being, so that it distracts the client. I am also talking about the nervy nature of the beginning, and the usefulness of respecting and allowing for that.

Even before therapist and group or client meet, many events may prejudice how each perceives the other. When a manager tells an employee he had better go for some counselling, this prescription may sound shaming or punishing rather than an attempt to be of use. When a doctor says to a counsellor that she can do nothing with a certain patient, so hopes the counsellor can get somewhere, the counsellor may feel some dread or hopelessness, before ever setting eyes on the person spoken of.

There are many many other pre-contact phenomena that will colour the first contact. Months and years are not available, in which to unravel whether an apparent surliness in the client at your first meeting is to do with something profound in her, or something superficial about the circumstances of your meeting.

Careful supervision helps guard against falling into counter-transferential swamps. The supervisee as well as the supervisor needs to be especially careful to examine her own processes as well as consider the larger field.

After fore-contact: contact

There are two major paths to choose from in BGT assessment. One path is to have a protocol for your work. This may well include a pre-meeting questionnaire (see Appendix A), range-scale forms, and some aid to careful formulation and diagnosis, such as that described later in this chapter. If such aids are used unthinkingly, no matter who the client or what his need, poor unspontaneous work will follow. Used with discrimination, they are likely to make for sensitive and thorough work by both people. As a rule of thumb, less experienced therapists may feel more confidence with some such aids. And there are many experienced workers who like to have mental checklists they can run. They claim that people unused to therapy often make a good beginning at thinking in new ways about their lives, as they fill in a pre-meeting questionnaire. Then they make better use of the short time in contact.

An approach demanding high skill is to rely on your ability as a therapist to make good sense of the absolute present, of what happens between you and the client when you meet. Using this path (Philippson, 1999), what is called **the structure of the contact** is the diagnostic tool. By this is meant constant comment on the flood of information generated by the being together of these two people or this group of people in these circumstances. The vignette from an assessment session with an offender, earlier in this chapter, gave an example of the use of the immediate impact of the client on the therapist, in affecting her breathing. After a quarter of a century of work as a therapist, the writer is generally at ease, and stimulated by this way of working, with most people. And there are others, perhaps whose own needs are for being cut-and-dried, with whom a more mechanistic beginning feels appropriate.

The beginning of therapy is likely to be more influential on outcome than later parts of it. What happens in the first seconds of meeting is likely to colour the whole episode of therapy.

In a first meeting, the patient may or may not have a sense of his **need**, of what he wants from the therapy. Not infrequently he will say that the doctor thought it might help, or that his manager sent him. Raising awareness of the nature of a talking therapy is thus an important early step. A willing patient may assume that he is to be a docile passive recipient of a Treatment, albeit one that requires from him a confessional input, as indeed would a visit to the doctor.

Client in charge

Learning something of the interactive and co-operative task the therapist has in mind will encourage some clients, and dismay others. **So, even in such a short episode of treatment, I recommend the therapist at the end of the first session to ask the client or patient to think over whether he wants to continue, and to get in touch about this in some specified way at or within an agreed time, but certainly not before having time to sleep on the decision**. If you use a pre-meeting questionnaire, it might well include a sentence such as:

> Some of what you write here may in itself help you think about your difficulties in a new way. It will also help us both decide if and how we can best work together when we meet. After our first meeting you will have until [named time] to decide if you would like to continue seeing [therapist's name] for the remaining [however many] sessions.

Many people have reported that this small device has helped them to feel committed and in charge of their own therapy. It also gives reflection time to the therapist, and an opportunity for her to refer the client on at this stage.

This is the exit of the first session. Before it comes, the hope is that the client has had time to describe what is troubling him, and to say what he wants from the therapy, if he can at this stage, and to form an impression of the therapist and her way of working.

On her side, the therapist does what she can to take on board the patient's way of looking at the world.

How you respond to each other

During assessment, as generally in the work, the primary focus of awareness in individual therapy for the Gestalt therapist is often most usefully on the I–Thou, on the quality of contact with the client. From this, and from the nature of interruptions to it, a tentative picture can be drawn of the likely work of most of the whole episode of therapy. Communicating this to the client, and negotiating the future work in the light of his reactions, begins the process of shared responsibility **which in itself constitutes part of the healing process.**

Mechanistic aids to assessment

It can be of great use to the therapist to be able to describe her insights, guesses and observations in a more I–it language and discipline, to herself, and perhaps in supervision. An aid to this is provided by Paul McHugh of Johns Hopkins University, in his book *The Perspectives of Psychiatry* (McHugh and Slavney, 1986). These perspectives are the framework for descriptive formulations, and are used in some of the foremost psychiatric institutions in the world. They are also so much in the spirit of Gestalt Therapy, in their holism and respect for the idiosyncrasy of each patient, that they are offered here. They are an aid to raising awareness of the field in which the patient perceives himself.

The new field of the therapist and patient as a system is attended to in the opening of dialogue, and the attention to the contact boundary outlined already. Assessment needs also to include an evaluation of whether the therapist is in her and her supervisor's judgement well enough suited to the needs of the particular patient. This may emerge partly from the first formulation, a method for which I suggest at the end of this section.

First, here are the foci, mostly on the other, which McHugh outlines. He recommends that proper attention is given to:

WHAT THE PATIENT IS This includes all that is readily measurable, such as age, marital status, position in family and so forth, to include general context and social history. In other words, these are the facts about, rather than the value given to them.

WHAT THE PATIENT HAS By this he means the symptoms, signs and difficulties the therapist is told or otherwise becomes aware of. In Gestalt language, these may often be perceived as characteristic of a contact style, reported, or in the here-and-now.

WHAT THE PATIENT DOES This is the here-and-now of behaviour, and the phenomenology generated in response in the therapist. It extends to cover patterns of behaviour the patient reports or demonstrates. Here are many clues about counter-transferential response, the way the therapist takes up the dialogue, and how else she might be of use to the patient. The whole examination of the client's contact style is referred to here. Does he agree eagerly wherever possible, suggesting confluence? Is deflection a major part of his style, or does he come across as a rigid introjector or a projector who sees the therapist in ways perhaps unfamiliar to the therapist herself?

WHAT THE PATIENT TELLS McHugh calls this the rich poem the patient has made of his life, to make sense of it. It is of great importance. But without attention to the other perspectives, it is insufficient background. Many narratives, for instance, are more revealing of a life attitude than of historical accuracy. On the other hand, sometimes they have historical accuracy, but seem discounted, devalued, by the teller.

He insists that it is never enough to pay attention only to one or two of these areas. Noticing all these perspectives means being as aware as possible of the whole of the person and one's first responses to him.

With awareness raised in these areas, the therapist can make a tentative plan about how to work. This is almost always talked over and if necessary negotiated with the client. As a way of learning this method, many students find it useful to write down one-paragraph answers to the following:

I notice:
Here are written concrete data, both the patient's history in the general sense, and the therapist's own phenomenological response.

I imagine:
This paragraph contains a formulation, or first guesses about what makes the patient tick, then what is imagined to be needed in the field, and how the therapeutic dialogue might best be focused – what needs to be kept as foreground.

I want:
Here is a first essay at an outline of what the therapist judges she needs to do, in the light of her suppositions about the other person. With few but important exceptions, this will involve negotiating and modifying ideas with the client, so that both can work together to raise awareness.

To illustrate some of this theory, here is the statement that Carol, a therapist, prepared for supervision after her first meeting with Amy, who was referred by her doctor for six sessions in a Primary Healthcare Centre.

Carol's four perspectives
WHAT SHE IS Amy is 52, married with two grown-up children. Her parents are both alive and she describes her childhood as normal. She works in local government, not in contact with the public.

WHAT SHE HAS She has a stutter that stops her speaking for several seconds at a time. She thinks she has always had it.

WHAT SHE DOES She is a churchgoer, chorister and gardener in her spare time. She dresses neatly in quiet colours and holds her handbag on her lap throughout the meeting. She has a cheque ready and folds it and puts it on the table rather than handing it straight to Carol.

WHAT SHE TELLS Her father has always worried about her stutter, and this Christmas gave her some money to get help with it. The stutter embarrasses her and makes her feel she is a bad person. She has chosen a quiet husband, she knows, so she will not have to talk too much. Singing releases her from the stutter and she belongs to a Bach choir as well as a church one.

The first organisation of data, or first gestalt formation

I notice Amy's formal way of sitting, her quick eyes and a slowness in agreeing with anything I say. I notice that I feel kind towards her, as if she needs reassurance. So I catch myself smiling even though she does not return the smile.

I imagine that she is quite fearful, and also that she does not want to have her world disturbed. She wants to keep the picture of nice parents, a nice husband and nice children, 'nice' being a word she uses often.

I want to work, at first, at least at the level of her behaviour, rather than motivation. In six sessions she can learn some mechanics. She may otherwise concentrate on resisting what she construes as probing.

Range scales

It would be possible to head this section 'Client task'. It is an aid to the clarity of all parties to the work, to help the client set up one or two, and certainly no more than three, range scales. These are lines marked off from 0 to 9, 0 signifying not at all, and 9 meaning very strongly. The client sums up a difficulty, states it, writes this above the scale, and marks where she feels she is on the spectrum at the moment. Then she marks in where she would like to move to eventually, and, perhaps in another colour or using a different symbol, where she assesses she might have shifted to by the end of the six or eight weeks of therapy. The therapist has much to do here, in eliciting statements, and checking the feasibility of the client's ambitions.

Amy had no difficulty in naming the reduction of her stutter as her construct. She put herself at 8 in terms of its present severity. She wanted it to be at 0 eventually, but thought that impossible. By the end of the six sessions she hoped to be at 6, a 2-point change. Carol asked if Amy would consider adding another construct – confidence – and mark herself on that. Amy was interested to do so, agreeing that she had very little confidence, and seeming surprised that this was either noticeable or worthy of attention. She put herself at 3 in confidence, hoping to move to 5 by the end of therapy, and 7 eventually.

This example shows one construct of symptom reduction, and one of attitudinal change, probably intimately connected to the symptom of the stutter. It shows how the therapist's observations and encouragement can be used to expand the client's ambitions for the therapy. In other cases, where foggy gestalt formation characterises the client's style, the eliciting of a construct is more difficult, and makes a worthwhile task for much of the first and/or the second session. In yet other cases, clients may need to be discouraged from the vaulting ambition to be new people with totally changed personalities after six or eight visits.

Symptom reduction is generally a negative ambition. Questions need to be asked, such as: 'How will your feelings be different? What will you do differently when [you are less anxious, sleep better, stop being so afraid, or whatever is the symptom that preoccupies the client]?' Constructs with positive ambition in them are often a better route to symptom reduction than keeping to the narrow gestalt of the symptom alone.

In group therapy, people can work in pairs to produce these range scales, after some encouragement to monitor each other in the directions suggested in the last paragraph. The results can be shown and talked about in the whole group, and perhaps modified in the light of feedback. Then partners can be chosen as weekday monitors, who agree to phone, email or in other ways communicate between sessions, to encourage work on the scales. The topic for the rest of the first session, or for part of the second session, is *How am I Going to Get There?* It is the time for setting up here-and-now experiments, demonstrations by others, plans for experiments before the next session, or whatever best suits the constructs presented. Some of these are likely to cluster, to overlap in ways that can reveal sub-groups of, say, undercontactful or overimpulsive people. These likenesses can become therapeutically useful, if some co-operation and even some rivalry sets up within the sub-group.

The different way in which these range scales are immediately constructed and used in individual and group work gives an indication of the particular incentives to excitement and growth, to useful comparison and sense of co-operation, that are possible in a group.

Summation

Respect and mutuality are central to BGT assessment. At best, the client or group will, by the end of the first session, have some clarity about how the therapist works, about an agreed focus of work, and about the trustworthiness of the therapist. Given time to reflect on the session before committing to the rest of the series offered, he will have a sense of being on his own terms rather than being exposed half-willingly to an imposed treatment. The work will have begun, whether through the telling of his story, the agreement on goals, the revelation of patterned responses, or experiments of other kinds.

Practice points

The tasks of the first or early sessions include:

Forming an impression of the contact boundary created between the two;

Focusing on the therapist's impression of whether she can create enough trust to allow a therapeutic bond to develop;

Finding out as much as she can of what the client has brought as a difficulty;

Filling out the client's impressions of the therapist and her task;

Formulating, in co-operation with the client, a first picture of what seems to make him tick;

Feasibility – coming to a tentative agreement about what aspect of the client's life or difficulty needs to stay foreground.

Appendix A

Examples of questionnaires that may be adapted for use before the first meeting of therapist and client:

1. Pre-counselling Awareness-raiser

An information sheet and questionnaire along these lines can be useful to both parties in Brief Gestalt Therapy. So here are reminders of some of the areas usefully covered in such a leaflet. Some agencies take failure to fill in such a form as an indication that counselling will not be of use. The reader's view on this and on many other points will dictate the content of any version of this questionnaire. A short statement of what counselling is about may usefully be added.

If information is given to the therapist by a doctor or someone else, then do not ask for that information again here. Part of the aim of this document is to befriend the potential client, rather than bureaucratise a system.

We hope that this paper will help you begin to think about the counselling that we can continue together for [X] sessions. It gives you a chance to reflect on some of your life and the ways that may be connected to what is troubling you at the moment. It is a help to the counsellor as well.

Anything you write (typed or in longhand) will only be seen by the counsellor and will remain confidential. The number on the form identifies it, so you do not need to write your name. When you have written as much as you want to, please return the paper in the confidential envelope provided. As soon as the counsellor receives it, she will get in touch with you to arrange a time to meet. If you find after reading this letter that you do not want to write anything, please get in touch in any case to make an appointment.

1. Please describe what has made you seek counselling at the moment.
2. Jot down other times when something similar has happened, or when you have reacted in this way.
3. (If necessary, make this an invitation to write something about present circumstances in terms of work and partnerships and so on, family history, how the client was brought up, parents' lives, and how these are like or unlike the client's. You may want to make several particular sections, such as parents, grandparents, siblings and so on.)
4. Are there any people to whom you can talk freely about your problems and about everything? How many?
5. What do you see as special successes in your life?
6. What change for yourself, perhaps in your feelings or ability to cope, or in some other way, would you like to work towards in our sessions together?

[These are examples of areas which you might ask people to think about before coming to see you. Then in the first session you can create between you some idea of the FOCUS and DIRECTION you agree.]

2. Brief Gestalt Therapy Pre-meeting Questionnaire

This is an example of an extended questionnaire. Some therapists find it useful. To others it is anathema.

This form is confidential and will only be seen by your counsellor.

The aim of brief therapy is to give you the chance to talk through what is distressing you, with someone who will not tell you what to do, but who wants to help you find your own way of coping, understanding or changing.

As this service can only offer [X] sessions, we hope that you will find time to fill out the parts of this questionnaire that apply to you, and return it to [X] by [time]. In this way we hope to save a little time, and also to give you an opportunity to think over how different experiences and people have affected you. Some of what you write here may in itself help you think about your difficulties in a new way. It will also help us both decide if and how we can best work together when we meet.

Please ignore any questions that do not apply to you.

If you need the help of someone else to fill out this form, please ask [X] at the practice. If you do not want to fill it out, but still want to meet the counsellor, please tell [X] in Dr [X]'s surgery and an appointment can be made.

[Space is left on the form for answering the following questions:]

1. Have you seen a counsellor here before? If so, please say approximately when and for how long.
2. Describe the difficulties that made you ask for help, saying how long you have had them, and when and where you first remember experiencing them.
3. How is your life at the moment affected by these difficulties?
4. What aspects of your life give you pleasure or satisfaction?
5. Have you or anyone in your family been referred to psychiatric or psychotherapy services before? If so, please give details.
6. Describe your general physical health. Have you had any serious illnesses or accidents?
7. Have you ever attempted suicide? If so, please outline the circumstances and what happened.
8. Are you taking any prescribed medicines at the moment? If so, please say what.
9. Are you taking any non-prescribed drugs of any kind?
10. Is there any concern about your drinking?
11. We would like some details about your family. First, how old is your father? If he is dead, how old were you when he died? What is or was his occupation?
12. Please answer the questions in 11. about your mother.

13. Now tell us something about your father's character or personality, and how you get on with him.
14. Tell us something about your mother's character or personality, and how you get on with her.
15. Please list your brothers and sisters in age order, including yourself, together with any stillbirths, abortions or miscarriages that you know about. Put the name and age of each, and your own age at the time any of them died.
16. Tell us something of your memories of your childhood, including any separations or big changes, as well as talking about other people who were important to you then, such as grandparents, aunts and uncles or others.
17. Are you single, married, divorced, widowed, separated, living alone or with a partner? How long have you been married or with a partner? What is his or her occupation?
18. If you do live with someone, do you have any difficulties in this relationship? If so, describe them.
19. Please list your children, including stepchildren, in order of age, including any stillbirths, miscarriages or abortions.
20. Please tell us something about your children.
21. With whom in your life do you have the closest relationship?
22. What do you find satisfies you, and what frustrates you, in this relationship?
23. Do you have any sexual problems or difficulties in sexual relationships? If so, please try to describe them.
24. What is your present home life? Is it difficult in any way?
25. Please tell us something about your social life. How do you respond to being in a group of people?
26. Please tell us something of your schooling and any later education.
27. What is your present occupation?
28. What are your plans and prospects in your work?
29. Please give a brief summary of the jobs you have had since leaving school, with dates, and details of what made you leave or change.
30. Describe any special satisfactions or difficulties you have had in your working life.
31. Please tell us anything else you think is relevant.

[Put a clear message here about how and when the first appointment will be made, its duration and confidentiality.]

Thank you.

4

The Beginning

Time needs to stay in the awareness of both parties to BGT from the beginning (Jacques, 1999). In many cases a fixed number of sessions are available, so the precise length of the available therapy is known. In other cases, both people start from the assumption that they will meet for less than so many weeks or months. This brevity can affect trainee therapists, making them stray into a hurry-up mode that probably ends by freezing both parties into immobility. Yet a great deal can and does happen in very short periods of time.

Some practitioners see clients in BGT for their six or however many sessions in a weekly sequence. Others vary the intervals between sessions, where this looks likely to be useful to the client. Holidays and other outside circumstances are one influence. A more potent one is the guess by both parties that an extended assimilation time between sessions will be productive, for this person at this time.

Some of the chapter headings in this book may suggest a neat programmatic set of stages in BGT. However, BGT is not a Procrustean bed to which any group or individual should be fitted. What is clear is that the emphasis in the work is likely to change in the light of how far the therapeutic journey has gone. Near the beginning there is likely to be more concern with how the past has formed the present. Towards the end, there will probably be more emphasis on what is wanted in the future.

It may be helpful, alongside the remorseless passing of time, to bring in the notion of **energy** as a constituent of the work. In the early days, Perls first called his new model 'Concentration Therapy'. By concentration, he meant high focus, high attention, the use of one's full powers, excitement or energy to let in the present and all its meaning. Marcel Proust (2000) contrasts this desired state with 'habit', as he describes his reaction to seeing a beautiful girl outside a train on which he was travelling:

> As a rule it is with our being reduced to a minimum that we live; most of our faculties lie dormant because they can rely upon habit. ... My habits, which were sedentary and not matutinal, for once were missing, and all my faculties came hurrying to take their place, vying with each other in their zeal, rising, each of them, like waves, to the same unaccustomed level, from the basest to the most exalted, from breath, appetite, the circulation of my blood to receptivity and imagination. (p. 220)

Such a heightened state is unlikely to be maintained by anyone for very long. The description is a reminder of what Perls perhaps meant by concentration. In some ways, it adds up to hastening slowly, and to paradoxical change itself, since that consists of no more than full acceptance and valuing of what is.

It is important at this early stage of the group or the pair, to create a field that can perhaps be called a **relevant totality**. The temptation for all parties may be to concentrate on dysfunction or distress. The healthy regard for self that brought the client to the consulting room is just one piece of available evidence that self-care and hope are somewhere in the field.

BGT has an implicit assumption that the client has a capacity for more satisfaction in life than he is likely to be experiencing when he first arrives for therapy. In the intensity of some crisis, therapist as well as client may, if not reminded, fall into a forgetfulness of the range of coping and enjoying abilities that are still there somewhere. The study of wellbeing has in the twentieth century taken a distant second place to the study of psychological illness. One count places the number of psychological abstracts since 1887 mentioning anxiety as 100 times greater than those mentioning life satisfaction (Myers, 2000: 56).

The second session

Whatever the intention, the reality of a second session is very often that the client spends a great deal of it filling out his story (Polster, 1987). This needs both to be listened to fully, and used as one side of the dialogue. The therapist also has the task, in these early stages, of doing all she can to achieve a clear **working alliance**. By this is meant an understanding between the parties of what they are there for and how they are going to set about their task. For the purposes of this book, it is a separate, though intertwined issue, from the **therapeutic relationship**. The working alliance concerns task. The therapeutic relationship concerns affect, or feeling and attitude. It is sometimes easier, when studying, to separate in order better to integrate these two aspects of brief or any other therapy.

> The clear working alliance can be difficult to reach, with someone full of worry and trouble, and unused to the ways of therapists. Training in BGT cannot overestimate the need to allow for the client's possible ignorance of therapeutic assumptions. In BGT, the therapist does not impose a therapy plan, but to a great extent either elicits one from the client, or negotiates one with him. Unless this is done at the beginning, it is likely that the best use will not be made of the episode of therapy by either party.

Aids to making a clear working alliance include the naming of the principal focus or foreground difficulty, and the setting up of range scales, both described and shown in Chapter 7. These show where the client sees himself now, where he would like ultimately to be, and where he thinks he might aim to be by the end of the brief therapy, in terms of his chosen focus.

This overt goal-setting and range-scaling are also advocated for groups. Participants can talk over their difficulties in pairs or sub-groups, draw their charts, and discuss them with the whole group. In the first session or two, they can set up any arrangements they can invent, for encouraging or monitoring each other between sessions. A spirit of co-operation is fostered in this way, often leading to friendships which last. These can be seen as an extension of the good therapeutic alliance hoped for in any therapy.

Very often a third of the time available for therapy is over by the end of the second session of individual work. Trust in each other and in the process is needed if the therapist is not to panic. She needs to remember that the client is likely to be working at least as hard as she is. If the client is not, then that in itself becomes the interesting figure. Self-sabotage has many meanings, all therapeutically relevant.

There are two large issues in individual or group BGT at this stage:

1. The diverse approaches needed for different people with different difficulties. For example, **being with** a recently bereaved person, without much active intervention except for empathic acceptance of him and his emotions, may sometimes be the surest aid to healing. Someone else, who seeks help, for example, with his tetchiness and inability to keep a job, and who perhaps lacks much insight, may need far more **doing**, by way of active experiments to illustrate to him what he does, and to let him discover what else he might do.
2. Except where crisis or trauma fill the foreground, some part of the beginning stages of the work involve **teaching**, albeit unobtrusively, about the assumptions and methods of BGT. These include the Gestalt aim of raising **awareness**, in the service of extending the client's **response-ability**, his ability to respond appropriately and flexibly. The other major focus in Gestalt, on the way **contact** – relating with others, including the therapist – is made or avoided, needs to be made clear. This email arrived at the writer's website, and seems evidence of the need for such teaching:

    As someone who is going to SEE a Gestalt therapist I have a question.

    I think the guy is really nice - I've been going for 5 weeks now but he never really says very much. I talk, he listens, I come home wondering what that was all about. He takes no notes, he gives little feedback and we dart from one thing to another - very much driven by me. I'm not sure what it's all about.

What should I expect from him? Every so often he will make a comment or ask me to describe how I'm feeling or how I felt about a certain thing etc but he doesn't offer suggestions on what to do about how I feel.

I have so many different things I'd like to discuss but it seems disjointed and lacking in structure and I'm left wondering whether or not he's sitting there wondering what he's going to have for tea. I don't think he does because he has referred back to previous sessions and seems to have remembered what I was saying.

Do you have any suggestions?

Yours faithfully

A rather confused client.

This is a communication that I hope would bring a deep blush to the cheeks of the therapist concerned. As Patrick Casement has explained with great lucidity, therapist and supervisor do well to learn from the client (Casement, 1985). From the start in BGT, the therapist needs to work towards an egalitarian climate in the counselling room, in a way that does not seem to have happened for the writer of the email. This is likely to make it easier for the client to express her confusion directly, rather than send off to a stranger for advice. It looks to me a strong potential piece of learning-from-the-client, to read from this client that by the fifth session, there may still be no shared understanding by both people of what they are there for. What is more, the emotional relationship between them has not made for confidence on the client's side. The result is that work has not properly begun.

Everything the client does in the therapy is potential learning for the therapist. If, for example, he often arrives late, that is a datum rich in potential information. There exist counsellors who are somewhat indignant at a client's bad time-keeping, and seek to discipline the client into regularity. In other words, they seek to suppress a symptom and win a power struggle. This sounds like self-importance, and also, naively taking a pre-designed role in the client's internal dialogue. It is likely to be of greater use to the client to find out what he wants from the lateness, how he achieves it, what effect he supposes it will have on the other, and whether he acts the same way outside therapy. In Perls's words, this is to analyse the resistance.

Other clients are reported to me, who manage to train their therapists into avoiding significant material from their lives. They do this by deflection, denial, refusal to speak of this or that, or by scaring the therapist. In doing this, the clients are truly training the therapist. The client will be better served if these attempts at training are viewed by the therapist as education. Training often seeks to elicit a response, without introspection or insight. Education brings forth, leads out. On the client's side, it brings forth his patterned interaction. For the therapist, it at best brings forth an awareness: **taking the role the client expects in a patterned interaction is more often than not a waste of therapeutic effort**.

Classically, Gestalt teaching follows, and is woven into, some happenings in the group or pair. In this way it is tied into reality, into the concrete. As soon as the hypothetical and out-there and abstract nudge into the group or pair, the therapist's job is to return to the present.

Dialogic method

One of the places where something near teaching is required in BGT is to do with dialogue. Existential-phenomenological dialogue (a phrase I hope would not be thrown at the head of a client) involves responding subjectively and honestly to what is said or provoked by the other (Buber, 1970; Friedman, 1990; Hycner, 1990). What this means is that instead of talking in abstractions and at opinion level, the speaker notices and reports the subjective phenomena that happen in response to the other. John McLeod (1993) gives an overview of the philosophical origins of the phenomenological approach that is a helpful introduction for people to whom this is a new method.

Here is an extract from an early session where the therapist attempts to respond dialogically, reporting sensations, memories, feelings and so on that are generated in her as she listens to Tim.

Tim, an imaginary client who gets sacked often, might talk as follows:

Tim: You see I get picked on all the time. I always land in the office where there's nasty people and they see me as the target.

Therapist: My stomach seemed to go cold, hearing that, and I'm going back over our meeting, working out if I've done anything that seems like picking on you.

Tim: Well, not so far you haven't.

Therapist: I see you sitting there, a big chap, big enough to scare me perhaps, if we met in the street. Yet when you spoke, your voice a bit tense, then I straightaway imagined a kid in a playground, who maybe wasn't in a gang, and got chased or something.

Tim: It didn't worry me. I gave them what for.

Therapist: I find I feel sad hearing that. You're telling me you weren't worried, and that you could cope. Then I feel sad. I want to know more about that.

Tim: I don't know what to say.

Therapist: Would it be easier to show me? Use one of the things in that bowl to be you, and the table can be the playground. Then find more objects to show the gang. Where are they?

At this point the dialogue has led to an experiment which turns out to show Tim's isolation and aggressiveness. The therapist's feelings and responses are set in, and modified by, the field of this being a session of therapy. They are often revealed as they happen, in the cause of raising the awareness of both people.

Rather than keep musings about the aetiology of Tim's troubles to herself, in BGT the therapist is more likely to bring in some of the therapeutic concepts that occur to her. Here she might talk about the Gestalt interest in the **significant missing element**. Tim's softer feelings are nowhere in evidence at the moment. Or she might introduce the idea of **polarities**: whatever is strongly present tends to be balanced somewhere by its opposite. In this case, he plays tough; the therapist feels compensatively vulnerable and sad. She might report this, and then ask if other instances of this pattern come to his mind. Or she might suggest that he finds a way, here and now, to notice opposite feelings in himself.

The introduction of theoretical concepts needs to be done with great discrimination. Novice therapists need to guard against getting carried away by the teaching role. Only what is highly relevant, and seems likely to help the client towards taking care of himself, is justified as information to be passed on to the client or group. Once again, jargon is an easy habit to acquire. Any good clear concept can be described in plain English too. Polarities is just a technical way of saying opposites. A significant missing element may be better taught by some ordinary question, as 'What's not there?' or 'What's missing?' By and large, nouns are to be questioned in BGT. They may be a fossilisation of what is better expressed dynamically, by a verb.

Openness with the client

Openness to the client is a prerequisite of any therapeutic method that produces good outcome. Openness with the client is a matter of far more disagreement between schools. Some methods foster careful abstinence in the therapist, in the expectation that this gives the client a clearer space into which to project, and show his tendencies in how he perceives people and works to make them respond to him. At best, this leads to insight for both people. Even people dedicated to this stance tend to modify it somewhat in brief therapy, since it is very likely in the early stages to make the client somewhat cross, bewildered or untrusting.

At the other end of the range are those therapists whose transparency is such that they are prepared to tell their own troubles and life events to the client. This activity is sometimes called sharing. Where I hear of it I require the sharer to substitute the word inflicting, and then reflect on what she notices. In other words, it is generally of dubious therapeutic value to crowd precious therapy time with the therapist's memoirs of weddings, theatre criticism and suffering relations.

From time to time the chime between the experience of both people is so precise that a harmonic will be generated usefully between them. An

I–Thou moment may occur in the revelation of, say, a dream dreamt by both people with similar content. This may melt into the trust, the being element of the relationship. It cannot be overstated that such divulging needs to be examined closely in supervision, to check whether it was an attempt at currying favour or pity, rather than a revelation of the therapist's increasing empathy or insight in the service of the client.

Holding boundaries

Trainee therapists often find it hard to deal with direct questions from clients, that apparently demand self-revelation. Are they to clam up, or blurt? Both responses seem likely to have a strong effect on the formation of a therapeutic bond. In Gestalt terms, the therapist needs at such a moment to hold a sense of the large gestalt. The field, the large gestalt, is, in the simplest terms, the client's presence to seek help with some named issue. Is knowing this or that about the therapist likely to take that task forward?

Here is an example of an almost 'out of the blue' question in a second session. Anne came to BGT from a workplace-counselling scheme. Her manager described her as touchy and difficult with colleagues. In her assessment session she spoke of rape by a family member during her 13th and 14th years. She said that this was the first time she had told about it outside the family. She insisted that this was all she could deal with in the six sessions allotted by the counselling scheme.

Anne: Have you ever been raped?

Therapist: That sounds to me a very important question. I remember you said how your mother told you to stop acting the tragedy queen when you told her about it, and refused to believe you. Now I imagine that you might be testing if I can possibly have empathy with you, in what you have described as a prolonged and insulting sort of torture.

Anne: But I just want to know.

Therapist: It's important to me to work with you so that you can lay that rape to rest, which is what you said you need to do. Comparing experiences can be very comforting. But your experience is unique. That's where I'm focused.

Anne: [*smiles brightly*] I'm really going to have my way, you know.

Therapist: This feels like a fight, with you determined to overpower me, and me cowering but trying to keep myself intact.

Anne: [*looking upset*] I did cower, right in the corner. But he got me. I don't want to be a kind of rapist too.

A large insight has come about. Like many vignettes of therapy sessions, this one shows a very strong experience. At worst, such quotations can suggest that all therapy is a string of such remarkable moments. In the author's experience, this is not at all the case. When and if something so vivid occurs in BGT, it may prove to be the pivotal event of the whole episode of therapy. It is a jolt to the spirit, and may well lead to what is described in Chapter 2 as a transformative experience.

This client's sudden insight into her own intrusiveness and need to overpower turned out to be much of what she needed. Over the following sessions, with frequent reference to this tiny episode in session two, she came to see how often since the rape she had dealt with people from the role of a victim or a rapist. In her own words, she either 'shrank from people or invaded them'.

Before leaving this quotation, it is worth remarking on not just the therapist's stance, but her choice of words. The client had earlier described herself as 'cowering', so that word was used again by the therapist. The word 'intact' was new to the conversation. The therapist used it as a true description of her experience, and at the same time with awareness of its virginal connotations. The haiku element of brief therapy is perhaps demonstrated in such precise language.

The rest of the therapy with Anne was a species of working through. She turned up each week with instances of how she had played victim or rapist, or of how she had invented some other style, in some instances to do with discoveries in the therapy. This was interspersed with some expression of rage at the original rapist, now dead. Copybook Gestalt Therapy might hope for Anne's letting go of some of the persistence of this bit of the past into the present. The actuality was that she concentrated far more now on how to be with people in more gratifying ways. The connection with the past was less often foreground for her after the second session. This makes for comment on two areas: assessment and the therapist's relation with any third party, here the employer.

Continuous assessment

In the first assessment session, Anne chose to focus on what she called 'getting over the rape'.

> *Therapist*: What is life like now, when you are not over the rape?
> *Anne*: So preoccupied about it. All sorts of feelings. A feeling of being dirty, and then feeling angry with him, and angry with myself for going on about it in my head.
> *Therapist*: In your head. Is there anyone you talk to about it, besides yourself?
> *Anne*: Absolutely no. Well, I'm talking to you. But I've withdrawn a lot from other people. I don't like that.

In other words, she did not make direct mention of the behaviour spoken of by the manager. The therapist accepted Anne's focus of their work, and also kept awareness of the touchiness commented by someone else, but not by Anne.

Her supervisor reminded the therapist that Anne's ways of dealing with people would certainly show in the consulting room. Either she would show her habitual ways of responding, and they would be available for comment. Or she would behave more co-operatively than reported, and that too would be grounds for comment. In other words, people can only behave as they usually do, or do something new or atypical.

The breakthrough in the therapy that is recorded here was a synthesis of Anne's focus and her manager's.

> *Anne*: It sounds daft, but I've been going about treating everyone as if they were that horrible man who raped me. Now I've talked him out of my system a bit, I'm starting to like people again. I've started smiling!

This can be seen as a lucky chance for the therapist, who for a short while could be 'all things to all men'. It is more likely that the connection between present behaviour and past trauma was so strong that this outcome was to be expected in a good piece of therapy.

It shows also how assessment needs to be constantly in the background if not the foreground of the therapist's awareness. It is not 'done and dusted' when there is an agreement about the focus of work in the early sessions.

To the reader this may begin to sound like a recommendation to slavish tracking of the client. On the contrary, in Perls's words:

> The 'endgain' must not be forgotten. It must remain in the field of consciousness. It must stay in the background, but guarding and planning the different 'means whereby' which are temporarily in the foreground. Under no condition must the 'means whereby' become isolated and lose their sense as means to an end. (Perls, 1992: 328)

The reality of the therapy quoted here can be described as, on the one hand, the client's wish to lay some of the **past** to rest, and on the other hand, the therapist's awareness of Anne's difficulties in getting on with people in the **general present**. It was likely, perhaps almost inevitable, that these would synthesise into some struggle with the therapist, **here and now**, like the one recorded here.

By keeping alert to the larger field, the therapist moved with the client into a more useful assessment of her present needs than the one first available to her awareness. If the therapist had held a fixed gestalt of this first, the laying to rest of the past, she might have sacrificed the valuable data in the absolute moment, for the sake of pursuing the stated agenda. She did not forget what Perls calls the endgain.

Relations with a third party

If a third party is concerned in the therapy, this needs to be dealt with, before any therapeutic agreement is made. If, for example, a young person living at home is brought to sessions by a parent or other, it is often important to talk to that person, probably in the presence of the prospective client, and establish an understanding about boundaries. Newly-fledged therapists sometimes show suspicion of such extra actors in the scene, if they ask how the treatment is progressing, or pass on their own views or experiences of the client. It is perhaps we therapists who are peculiar in requiring confidentiality, rather than the family members who have since time immemorial embarrassed their relations with public musing about them.

Tact and sympathy are needed from the therapist, in the hope of ensuring that the third party has some understanding of the advantages of confidentiality, and some assurance that he or she will be told if there is any crisis that needs their intervention. If this person is alienated, he or she will likely talk disparagingly to the client about the therapist and therapy in general, and so tend to undermine what is being built in the consulting room.

There is widespread ignorance of what therapy or counselling are about, and plenty of mistrust too. The whole episode of treatment will be greatly affected by the way referral happens, as was talked of at length in the last chapter. So the therapist will do well to see what she can do to make this effect beneficent.

In the instance quoted in this chapter of workplace counselling, power relations might well militate against good therapy. A cross manager might in part want to discipline or humiliate by making a recommendation for counselling. The client might respond with understandable bad will. The therapist might feel beholden to her employer, who is also the client's, and feel bound to work on the manager's agenda rather than Anne's.

There needs to be an oral agreement between the therapist and the organisation, and preferably a written document, which deals with:

1. Who is to be referred;
2. How they are to be referred;
3. How confidentiality is to be defined;
4. Whether supervision is to be offered or paid for by the agency;
5. Who in the organisation will respond to the therapist;
6. Who will pay for the therapy, how and when.

Setting up a briefing meeting or two with relevant staff is usually effective. It is a chance for everyone to gain more awareness of each other's needs. A specimen contract is offered in the appendix to this chapter.

In Employer Assisted Programmes (EAP) work, the funding organisation sometimes imposes its own contract. Rather than simply signing on the dotted line, BGT therapists are recommended to see how far they are at ease with the conditions, particularly around note-taking and confidentiality, that are required of them. Asking for meetings, crossing out clauses, talking to someone on the phone, are a few of the ways in which the therapist can bring modifications to the contract, or at least cause it to be reviewed in the future. Form-filling through most of a first session, notifying people in his workplace of the alcohol intake of the client, and so on, are sometimes dubious ethical procedures. Because such work can be well paid, there may be a temptation to conform to the conditions imposed. This is a warning to do otherwise.

Unfortunately, the word counselling is used to describe one stage of the disciplinary procedure that can lead to dismissal from the workplace. Any overtones of punishment need to be removed from people's minds. In the same way, promises of instant reward are not likely to be useful. A well-meaning lecturer may tell a student that he will be sure to like their wonderful Mrs Bloggins, who helped another student amazingly in similar circumstances. Such pre-judging is perilous and to be discouraged.

At the other end of the spectrum, some politicians have fostered the notion that all bad events in people's lives should be followed immediately by – note the same word – counselling. The truth seems to be that some severely distressed, traumatised people do need to talk to or be with a sympathetic stranger for some sessions. Others will cope far better by rest or by talking to their friends and families. These are examples of referral criteria that will probably need to be made clear to teachers, lecturers, managers, surgery staff or others.

It can be hoped that these people can also be taught to pick out psychotic behaviour that is best dealt with by instant referral to psychiatric help. And in the workplace it may be worth talking through, and largely discouraging, any hopes a manager has that therapy equates to career training.

How people are referred includes whether much, if anything, is to be said about them to the therapist without their knowing. This is for negotiation between each therapist and agency. Some therapists want to start with a *tabula rasa* with all clients. Then again, particularly in doctors' practices, medical notes are assumed by all parties to be shown to professionals. This may be acceptable to clients as well as helpful to the therapist. Or it can be proscribed at the outset.

The agency staff on their side need to feel confident that people will not find the sessions useless. They need to have some idea of what is involved in BGT, along with an explanation that it is not a career advisory or housing or other service.

Whatever the written agreement, it can happen that exasperated managers or frustrated lecturers want to use the therapist as an itching post for their own grievances about the person to be referred. Therapists need to avoid confluence with their clients' view of the world. Equally, they need to stay clear of being over-influenced by such third parties. There is an art in registering, rather than rubbishing or reverencing, what is said about a client. The therapist in the episode with Anne gives an example of how this can be done.

Practice points

The BGT therapist will always be characterised by her attention to awareness, contact and response-ability, and by the methods of phenomenological dialogue and experiment.

Sensitive attention to the moment as well as to the strategy of intervention is designed to create and maintain a respectful and honest therapeutic bond as soon as possible.

Time is in the therapist's focus, even if the client seems to have entered a zone of timelessness.

The larger field of how people are referred needs attention from the therapist, if the best conditions of entry into the work are to be offered to clients coming to therapy from agencies.

Appendix B

Contract between therapist and third party

[Client name]

Referred by: [name of third party]

[Therapist name, address and work phone number]

[Therapist's professional association, by whose ethical code (enclosed) she works]

Length of contract: [X] sessions lasting [X amount of time] each.

Person in organisation to whom therapist should refer in emergency: [name]

Payment per session: [amount]

Person in organisation to whom invoices should be addressed, after each session or at end of each month: [name]

The therapist works on the understanding that what goes on between her and the client is confidential, except in the unusual circumstances outlined in the attached ethical code.

The client is not bound by the rules of confidentiality that govern the therapist. Practice has shown, however, that most people prefer not to be asked about their therapy, particularly by people in authority in the organisation.

The therapist is more than willing to come and talk to interested managers or other relevant people, on the general topic of who is best referred for therapy from within the workplace, and how. Please feel free to get in touch about this, or anything else you would like to know about this work, to arrange a meeting time.

5
The Middle

What I am calling the middle is the part of BGT that follows after an agreement has been reached about the focus of the work. Reaching this agreement includes establishing trust, and what is here termed 'therapeutic relationship', as well as a working alliance.

Generally, the middle is likely to stretch from about the third session, through as many as are available before the therapist, if not the client, notices that the end is close enough to need to be dealt with. In this middle phase, people will change subtly as time passes, as a leaf changes colour and texture through the summer. At best, this change will be a maturing rather than an atrophy of the relationship between therapist and client, or between group members, including the therapist.

Whether or not the client or group members are able at the time to feel regard and respect for the therapist, her work is to behave in ways that are worthy of respect and trust. Compassion, patience and the honest desire to understand probably transmit to some part of the client's mind and are available there to be recalled. Faith may be needed to sustain the stance recommended here, at times when no direct gratification is offered by a client. Mander (2000: 51) sums this up, and highlights some of the qualities needed as much in this as in any other phase of BGT. What she describes here is two-plus-one-session therapy:

> The secret of therapeutic effectiveness in this briefest of modes lies in a combination of quick and clear thinking, of intuitive hypothesising and instant rapport that allows for a shift in the context of relating and engages the patient in an emotional experience that constitutes a clinically relevant change, some new understanding, some behaviour modification, a measure of affective relief.

With most groups and clients, the progress of trust and risk-taking and ability to appreciate self and other are clearly evident as time passes. This growth of the freedom to be oneself in the presence of another is probably the most potent aspect of BGT or any other brief or long-term therapy. Attention to and appreciation of a progress charted for everyone concerned in:

(a) the relaxing of tension;
(b) the increasing readiness to confide; and
(c) an increased capacity to enjoy and to react spontaneously

is often the most important focus for the BGT therapist through this middle phase of growth and unfolding.

The therapist's other continuous focus needs to be on the client's stated areas of work, as depicted probably on range scales. Some clients will digress and deflect in all directions from these one or two foci if the therapist is confluent. Skill is needed to keep the foci in the foreground, by other than draconian or schoolteacher admonishments.

The following vignettes may illustrate one or two ways of achieving what is described:

> *Client*: [*in third session. Her stated focus is to make a better relationship with her teenage stepson and daughter.*] My aunt says she's coming to stay, and that makes me so annoyed. Why can't she stay in a hotel? She doesn't even like me. I've got to talk about that today.
>
> *Therapist*: Yes. We can look at your feelings about this aunt, and see what clue they give to your side of how you get on with these other relations, the stepchildren.

Or

> *Client*: [*in fourth session. His focus is how to manage his tendency to depression.*] Well, we've licked the depression, thank you very much. So I thought we might move on to having a look at my catastrophic choice of girlfriends. I just met someone last night, and I can feel the old familiar signs of falling madly in love.
>
> *Therapist*: You're seeing a link between that and what you called the management of your depression?
>
> *Client*: No, no. The depression's fine. This is different.
>
> *Therapist*: I'm noticing the connection, in time if nothing else, between your mood change and finding someone attractive, someone you also think may be a catastrophic choice.

Both these vignettes are meant to show how clients often have fragmented perception, and do not see the connections between different parts of their lives, and their difficulties. Supervisees not uncommonly in my experience are mesmerised into the same fragmentation, and find it difficult to see that they can deal with the same issue from whatever standpoint the client takes. The analogy is with dreams, which often seem to present one dilemma through several apparently disconnected scenes.

The theory of paradoxical change is dear to the hearts of many Gestalt practitioners. This belief that self-acceptance can in some almost miraculous way immediately make change possible is borne out in Gestalt Therapy, and indeed in person-centred counselling. In brief work, it seems especially useful to remember that both Fritz and Laura Perls assumed other routes to change to be possible as well.

Experimenting with opposite behaviour, for instance, is not the same as recognising and embracing the dominant present style. It is a deliberate move away from it. The neural paths that have been forged and reinforced are thus by-passed, in the cause of creating or reinforcing others. While for some people the middle phase of brief therapy will best be used in gaining the self-love and confidence that go with paradoxical change, for others, all manner of deliberate experiments may move them in the direction they have chosen. Someone with a tendency to violence, for example, may benefit most in therapy from raised awareness of just what triggers violent behaviour, and when.

Therapist: So it's when someone looks at you in a certain way across a pub that you do what you call just going mad?

Client: They might not mean a thing, I don't even know them, but I churn inside, and I've just got to glass them or thump them, like now!

Therapist: Let's picture the scene. How crowded is the pub?

Client: Yeah. It's quite a few people, I'm better if it's quieter, that's right.

Therapist: So it's a crowded pub. And noisy, you're saying. How far away is this person who might look at you?

Client: Not sure I want to start imagining that. In fact I might walk right out of here if you start making me do that.

Therapist: Now you're helping me with another idea. See if you can imagine a safe kind of place you'd like to go to if you did walk out of here or out of that pub.

Client: My girlfriend took me out to Epping once; it was all woods and the sun coming through the leaves.

Therapist: Notice how you feel when you remember that place.

The memory of something peaceful that can be revisited in imagination is built on for much of the session. It will serve as a retreat or asylum when the client feels too much anxiety in the work of exploring his low violence threshold, and raising it to a safer level.

So, the idiosyncrasy of people who seek therapy, the diversity of what they bring, and the differences in style from therapist to therapist, mean that there will not necessarily be a similar middle phase of each episode of therapy. Someone coming through postnatal depression while looking after a first baby is likely to need a quite different middle phase of BGT from someone else, who is perhaps wanting the skills to deal less aggressively with people at work.

What is likely to be common to this period of the work is an element of consolidation. This is likely to be on two fronts. One is the content level of dealing with perceived difficulties. The other is the process itself of being with the therapist.

On the one hand, a depressed young mother may in BGT begin to notice and enjoy the unconditional interest and concern the therapist shows her. This at best will help give her the confidence to begin to feel and show some of the same in her other new relationship, and come nearer to enjoying the mothering role with her baby.

In another instance, the short-tempered employee may be able to learn from the novelty of talking to someone who for once in her life does not retaliate, but investigates with her the content, the mechanics of what triggers her attacks. At the same time, at process level she may begin to relax, to change her contact style. Recent research into mirror neurons (Gallese and Goldman, 1998) gives evidence of even more complicated physiological responses in interaction than we could witness before. In the middle phase of BGT, these at best will happen in an atmosphere of much less fear than many clients habitually experience.

At the content level, she may well be one of those who will benefit from experiments that let her grasp more clearly the feelings and trigger responses she has. Later experiments may then be in the nature of rehearsals of new contact styles she wants to have in her repertoire.

> Wilfred Bion (1961) spoke of two groups being present in any one group: the Task Group and the Affect or Emotional Group. Some of the same holds for the therapeutic pair. Very often indeed, if the emotionality of the system does not work properly, neither will the task.

There is a corollary to this. If the task is going very well, that will probably of itself generate good feeling. On occasion, an apparently busy therapy, with more do than be, so well suits that client that there is trust and respect and a generally enhancing state of feeling.

The task for the therapist, or much of it, is to use her best powers to enter the world of the client, to see it as he does, without losing her own perspective. This is a process of contact and withdrawal, carried on constantly and largely out of awareness. The shorthand word for it is empathy, or for Yontef (1993), inclusion. At best, it will also have some of the love Latner (1982) speaks of, and which Rogers (1961) more obscurely terms unconditional positive regard.

Caring, however, is not a substitute for coping. Excellent rapport, without diagnostic acumen and other task competences, does not constitute therapy.

The experiment

In the context of Gestalt Therapy and BGT, an experiment is an activity, probably invented on the spur of the moment, that seems likely to further the therapy. It may be a piece of imagining, as in the example above of the creation of a safe asylum. It may involve movement or speech, or be undertaken in BGT as something to try out between sessions.

Much of this chapter is an attempt to raise awareness of the range, the kind and the intention of some of the experiments that are part of BGT. The background to this chapter has to be a high awareness that Gestalt Therapy is very much concerned with spontaneity and immediacy.

> The experiment is the cornerstone of experiential learning. It transforms talking about into doing, stale reminiscing and theorising into being fully here with all one's imagination, energy and excitement. (Zinker, 1977: 123)

Moreno (1946) was the original thinker behind most of what have come to be called experiments in Gestalt. In BGT they are often of immense worth in illustrating a block to awareness and action, or allowing a way through that block.

The caveat that needs always to be there is that the greatest value needs to be accorded to the dialogue – the between – that is generated in this group or between these two people in this unique moment. So the experiments that are described here are not intended as ready-packaged, ready-to-serve, shrink-wrapped items to be pulled out of the therapeutic shopping bag with scant regard to context.

Introducing experiments

Another caveat is to do with how experiments are introduced. John Frew (1992) spoke at a conference of three categories of intervention in Gestalt Therapy group leadership. These are: (a) to impose on; (b) compete with; or (c) confirm.

Most of the time, imposing adds up to overpowering, or not allowing the power of the other to be engaged. It is a poor way to introduce an experiment. Force provokes force; imposition provokes resistance, or resigned submission. It is a facet of what has come to be called oppressive practice in all psychotherapy. It is power-over.

Competing is on occasion a dysfunctional expression of something that is otherwise recommended here – a horizontal relationship. It is power-against, stemming from fear of the rival. In BGT, it may show in redundant use of psychological jargon, which says covertly, I'm smarter than you are. It may surface as an apparently wise and friendly invitation to do or say this, that or the other which carries the meaning, I'll show you who's boss around here.

Co-operation, mutuality and co-creation are more desirable in Gestalt experimenting. Whoever is the subject of an experiment needs to agree to it freely before beginning.

It is unwise, for example, to say to someone, 'Exaggerate that movement', before making some preface and seeking permission, perhaps saying, 'I notice you tucked your hands behind your back as you spoke. Do you want to see if we can find out more about that?'

Working in this way makes clear that the therapist is in a service role to the client. It does nothing for therapist grandiosity and the wish to impress. Gestalt is not abracadabra therapy.

Making sense

Triggers to experimentation stick out all over most therapeutic conversations. A mutter invites the possibility of reversing to a clear statement or even a shout. A bitten lip can be seen as a silent intrapsychic dialogue between an attacker and part of the organism that is attacked. And so forth. But if all these triggers are pulled, the therapy may begin to sound like random small-arms fire.

The job of the therapist is in part to stay aware of context. Attempting to plunge nervous new clients into what to them may seem a most bizarre piece of behaviour is to ignore the ground. Going along with yet another cathartic experience for someone whose deficit is in thinking, or going along with another intellectual exploration for someone whose deficit is in emotional expressiveness, is likewise to ignore the ground. The therapist's role is seldom to reinforce established patterns of behaviour, but more generally to explore new ones, and extend the client's repertoire of response. In Gestalt jargon, this makes response-ability, leading to fluid and appropriate response in the world.

A useful attitude for the therapist to hold and to encourage in the client has to do with 'What do we know so far? What are we discovering now?' This is not a matter of prior knowledge, ready-made assumptions or prejudices, or overconfident prediction. Talking through the meanings **for the client** of any experiment is generally very important indeed.

Talking through

The have-over is the term sometimes given to the thorough talking through that can usefully happen after an experiment, whether in one-to-one or group work. The word dialogue of itself means no more than talking through, talking over thoroughly, whatever the refinements of meaning we have imposed on it since the time of the Greeks.

Much of the value of an experiment may be lost if this talk does not happen. Likely insights may leap quickly to the mind of the therapist or some participants. Other people need a longer chewing-over time, to extract their own meanings from what they and others have done.

Without some discipline, this talk can turn into amateur psychoanalysis, meandering anecdote or advice sessions of dubious value. A number of questions are pertinent here, some more appropriate to one occasion, others to another. Readers may have suggestions or questions of their own to add or substitute to these. The underlying principle is to do what can be done to make an unthreatening exploratory atmosphere. At best, this will foster curiosity and discovery, rather than shame and blame.

Feedback topics

All I can do is repeat what I tend to do and feel, or find something new. To help people chew over and find more nourishment in what has just happened in an experiment, some of these questions are often of use:

> What did I like about what I did or felt?
>
> How did what I did in this experiment resemble what I do at other times?
>
> What scenes from the rest of my life come into my mind as I talk over this experiment?
>
> What was new about what I did?
>
> Notice the feelings and attitudes of the other players in those scenes, as well as my own.
>
> What do I want to change about what I did?
>
> What is the one step towards change I can take now, this minute? Do it. Talk it over in terms of sensation, emotion, assimilation.

Every experiment can be successful

Supervisees sometimes report that they suggested an experiment, 'But it didn't go anywhere.' There is **always** something to be learned from the process of an experiment, for the therapist, if not for the client, and generally for both. Here is an example:

Hal is aged 34, and has been referred for brief therapy by his doctor. He is off work after his female partner left him. He wants, in his own words, to 'get his life together again'. This is the second of six sessions.

Therapist: As we talk I keep noticing how you've made a fist of your right hand, and keep punching into your left palm. Oh, you've stopped doing it.

Hal: Have I?

Therapist: And now you've put both hands in your pockets.

Hal: Since they seem to upset you.

Therapist: Upset?

Hal: Well now, what would you like me to do?

Therapist: To notice connections maybe. [*She decides, interested in his irritation, that it may seem too contentious to point out just now that Hal is in charge, or that she has not ever asked him to do anything, or any other fact that might be seen as, or be, an escalation of the argument between them.*]

Hal: Oh, for God's sake! So this fist hits that hand, so I'm beating myself up; well, we knew that, it's why I came to see you.

Therapist: Yes. [*She broods about whether to add, 'And now you are beating me up instead'. The pause lengthens.*]

Hal: I'm sorry, I'm very frustrated and I lash out. I know I do. But I'm not going to do any of these play-acting things I've read about in Gestalt, and that's that.

Therapist: So here you are, too devastated, that was the word you used last week, too devastated to go out or go to work. And you have got it together, got just enough hope, to turn up to see me. And now you are here something makes you – if I used a physical simile, I'd say – push me off.

Hal: Are you trying to say I've got to play by your rules?

Therapist: I find myself thinking about your Anna who left you, and wondering if you picked fights with her.

Hal: All the time. She said I'd got to have life on my terms. She was right, actually.

By the end of the session, Hal has gained insight into some of the fear behind his dictatorial manner. The experiment has 'gone somewhere', though the route has not been that perhaps first imagined by the therapist.

It needs to be noted that it is easy for therapists to be a little blinkered or a little stubborn themselves, and want an experiment to unfold on their terms. So, 'going nowhere' sometimes means 'not going my way'. The heart of the matter is that notice is taken of, and value is given to, whatever happens, whatever develops in the session, and the client is encouraged to make his own sense. This sense may well be fleshed out by observations and perceptions from the therapist, as above.

Categories of intervention and experiment

We can assume that experiments will be done with many people at times through the middle phase of BGT. To give some sense of what belongs where, we can separate in order to integrate. We can look at experiments in temporary categories, even though categorisation does not live long or often in harmony with holism, which is the ultimate objective in BGT. These categories overlap even in description, and when experiments from whichever standpoint are carried out, the effects are likely to be observable across the board, or throughout the organism. But for study purposes, we suggest that Gestalt experiments often begin from particular therapeutic perspectives, some of which are described under the following sub-headings.

Diagnosis or trawling

This may, especially in a group, be the first kind offered.

All therapist interventions can be seen as potentially diagnostic. From the response they elicit, they reveal more than was so far known about the client, and probably about the therapist as well.

Many people are well aware of the distress that brings them into therapy. Others are far less articulate about what connects their behaviour, feelings, history and general context.

One of the many ways of working with people who look outwards more than inwards, or are somehow not fluent about their own psyches, is to propose what I here term a 'trawling' experiment. Perls mentions this process in *Gestalt Therapy Verbatim* (1969: 130):

> He invites a group, as an individual therapist might well invite an individual, to sit quietly with shut eyes and imagine a dialogue with their own dreams. The outcome of the experiment is clear: to discover more about the dreamers' attitudes to their dreams, and to make an opportunity for changing those attitudes if that is wished.

This experiment is not about the content of any one dream. It is about one person's dreams, as if they were an entity. Neither is the experiment a response to the expressed need of everyone present. It is an example of doing something likely to show participants something more about their perceptions, and their responsibility for their own experience.

People sent for, rather than actively seeking, therapy, sometimes do not know how, or do not want, to begin. That state needs to be respected and dealt with in patient dialogue. Once there is a willingness to begin, some experiment involving projective elements may help focus. Looking at Tarot cards, pebbles, brands of car, or whatever catches the imagination of the client, and describing oneself in terms of likeness and unlikeness to one or two, or aversion and attraction to them, is an example of how to begin when there is apparent ignorance of what therapy is about and how it can help the people present.

A more elaborate exercise about blocks (Houston, 1998a) is described in greater detail in Appendix C, along with one or two others from the great range of what can be created in this category. Readers may have their own favourites. Many of the warm-up exercises used in psychodrama groups have the same quality as these above, in that they tend to generate activity, interest, focus on different sensory modalities, and therapeutic discoveries.

Experiments that concretise

Life is a series of small scenes. The last suggestion in the Feedback topics section was a direct lead into such a small scene. A resolution, for example, to 'be nicer to people', or 'stand up for myself' may well be envisaged as a sincere wish – somehow connected to the middle distance – of next Sunday, or at work, or whatever. Very often there can be an experiment taking only a few seconds that embodies the general wish, and makes it instantly concrete. In a group there will certainly be scope for an immediate, 'being nice' or 'standing up' to someone or other. Tried out and commented on, this will consolidate a group member's discoveries or skills, and probably add more. 'How could you experiment with that here?', 'Has anyone else ideas of what Y might do?', 'Do you want to try that, Y?' and 'Check if X is willing to work with you' are questions that may be of use.

Emotional insight

When a client has awareness of what Perls might call a hole in his personality, or a gap of skill in handling the world, there may be a case for finding out more about the background of this blank. If a developmental block or deficit, manifesting emotionally, is the stopper, then work may well be directed there.

With some clients, fostering emotional insight can usefully be most of the work of BGT. People not uncommonly come to therapy deeply puzzled about what they see as their irrational responses to other people or the world. For some of them, understanding how their difficulty began, or what it stands for, is enough to allow change and comparative peace of mind.

It needs to be said too that some people demand insight, only to use it as an embellishment to their wooden leg. Many of us have come across the person who says, 'I know I run up awful debts and my poor husband has actually got ill with worry. But I can't help it. My therapist says it's because I had such a deprived childhood.' Simply helping people to account for their antisocial behaviour is not necessarily good therapy. Raising awareness of how change can be effected is also part of the work.

Very often people are straightforward in believing or indeed knowing that if they can make sense of their behaviour, they will be free to change it. For them, investigating the way the past, or more precisely, the feelings and attitudes they have preserved from the past, are intruding on the present and even blighting it, will be useful work indeed.

A sensitive therapist will do much of this work by commenting on the process in the consulting room. The feelings that are generated in both people, and the behaviour, are a rich source of insight about old introjects and much else. From this conversation, more formal experiments will usefully be generated.

Two chairs

The two-chair dialogue is the best-known and potentially most effective of these. This experiment is known and respected for its proved efficacy (Clarke and Greenberg, 1986; Conoley et al., 1983). It is described in some detail here, because familiarity sometimes breeds carelessness. In contemporary Gestalt Therapy it is sometimes less used, so the way it is introduced and developed is probably worth commenting on here.

This is one of the experiments more likely to be suggested by the therapist than the client. Very often, the conflict inherent in the material seems to keep the split out of the client's awareness. Indeed, sometimes the client who says he is going to do a two-chair exercise, and arrives prepared with the subject of it, will simply give a performance of something that has been rehearsed at home or in other settings, and is of limited therapeutic value unless the therapist is very nimble.

Here is a checklist for conducting a two-chair dialogue. It does not name many subtleties of intervention, but is meant as a reminder of much of what needs as a rule to be lived out. Circumstances alter cases, and you may need to do more or less than what is outlined here. Part of the reason for putting this list here is my observation that even experienced practitioners sometimes make very partial and inadequate exploration of this way of working.

Checklist for conducting a two-chair dialogue

- Check that the subject wants to work.
- Say again the names of the two polarities that provoked the idea of two-chair work.
- Ask which polarity is experienced more in the place where the person is sitting. Encourage present investment in that, in fantasy and physical attitude and feelings.
- Invite statements to be made from that place to the other polarity, imagined on the other seat.
- Check if the subject is ready, and if so, suggest she moves to the other seat and now takes on the attributes of that polarity.
- Remind her of the statement just made to her from the other seat. Invite her response, in her feelings and statements.
- Continue to suggest movement back and forth between the chairs, as the client dictates, for instance by losing energy in one place, or by beginning to speak as if from the other, before she has moved.
- If the dialogue stays in blame, or resignation, or otherwise sticks, ask the client what the polarity she is in needs from the other, or would like to offer the other. In other words, see if there is scope for change.
- If there is not, the therapist may do well, rather than cajoling, to comment that this is the outcome of the experiment. The discovery has been made that the client chooses for now to hold firmly to the attitudes she has.
- If change does show, that can be explored in the two-chair dialogue until a new integration is experienced by the client.

After an intense two-chair dialogue, check if the client needs to sit quietly and settle with what she has done and learnt, or whether she is open to hearing back from other people, if the work happens in a group.

Missing modalities and missing stages

Long ago, a trainer asked me to describe a stranger who had just driven up fast to the verandah where we were working. When I had done so, he said, 'And what is she like?' He was not at all impressed with my answer, and said, 'You get all the data, but you do nothing with it'. This brings to mind Sherlock Holmes's comment to Dr Watson, that *he saw, but did not observe.*

Since then I have noticed how often people do this. They or I take in the data, but do not allow a new organisation that gives an insight. Habits of politeness or conventions about character judgements come between what is observed, and what is concluded.

Most of us have come across the client who repeatedly pairs with the wrong person. Sometimes they are as I was, and seem to have baulked at making sense of the evidence to their senses. Others seem to have selective sight or hearing or memory, and do not hold very large awareness of this other person, or perhaps of themselves (Maibaum, 1992). They are some of the people for whom sensate experiments may be rewarding.

Listening to a piece of orchestral music several times, focusing on each occasion on a different instrument, may be a valuable flanking approach to such a difficulty. In other words, they are, in a way probably unusual for them, deliberately seeking and staying with a connected set of data. Finding if and how attention lapses, or confusion sets in, is valuable information in itself.

Experiments that invite an open receptivity to sight or sound can also help some people to a more general openness to what is novel. Another form of listening, for example, is to allow into awareness the fact that sound enters the whole body, though most of us construe it as only to do with the ears. Sitting or lying at ease and noticing the responses to music that happen throughout the body is another sensate exercise that could be highly educative for people whose contact style is tense and controlling. Such people may operate for preference through verbal reasoning and intellectualising.

Experiments like these described just here take some time, and might be an assignment to work on between therapy sessions. In the cause of hastening slowly, they may profitably sometimes be the content of a middle session of brief therapy.

Most of us sum up passages of our holiday or job or childhood as 'moments-when'. The moment when a gift was given, or something startling or gratifying happened, was probably both formative in itself, and the mnemonic for a whole chapter of experience. In Brief Gestalt Therapy, if one moment from the five or eight or twelve or twenty sessions remains in someone's memory as a clear gratification, that may well be an indication of success. It is likely to have the quality of what Perls called a mini-satori, an awakening or transformative experience.

Rehearsal and model-building

People who do not give much attention to their psyches may profit more from experiments that let them try out new behaviours than from more introspective work. People who do feel their feelings and seek insight will almost certainly need some education as well about how to handle quarrels or love affairs or authority, or whatever area is the threatening one for them. It is perhaps useful to remember that most of us have gaps in our social skills, or in some area of dealing with the world.

On occasion it can be important to let someone slowly build up a model of how to do some operation that other people may consider childishly simple. For example, most people understand that rehearsal is worthwhile before such things as formal job interviews. This is to a great extent because these are rare events for which we probably have a low skills base.

But some people have rarely been to a party and found a way to be its life and soul, or even to preserve a decent sense of their own worth while there. Others find dealing with rude shopkeepers or waiters a cause of humiliation. Setting up role-plays in which the protagonist can watch a more confident person take her role is one route to building a strong internal model, an RIG (a Repeated Interaction that is Generalised) in Stern's (1985) terminology. When the adequate performance has been commented on, or repeated by yet another group member, then the protagonist may play the part herself. In the feedback talk, attention can be given to body posture, breathing, movement, voice tone and the other accompaniments of speech, until the protagonist has embodied the new learning to her satisfaction.

Embodiment

In the short time available in this sort of therapy, the therapist will be keen to make the most of it, and draw as much meaning as she can from each session. In a speech-dominated society, much of the work of BGT is likely to be verbal. Yet in many of the experiments already mentioned in this chapter, there will be more than words. In a two-chair dialogue, the client may find out an enormous amount simply by taking on in turn the physical attitudes of the two sides. In almost any experiment, paying attention to what was behind a gesture or drying up or change of position may be an illuminating moment.

Here is a fragment from the fourth session with Amy, the middle-aged client with a stutter, whose range scales are described in Chapter 3.

Carol: It looks to me very difficult to speak on an in-breath, and that's what you keep doing. What happens if you take a breath sharply again, but this time just notice your feeling, rather than trying to talk?

Amy: [*Experiments*] Fear. Awful fear, really. [*She experiments again, and this time the word 'Don't' sounds through the in-breath.*]

Carol: 'Don't.' With your eyes staring and such a look of terror. How old do you feel as you say that?

Amy: About seven, I think.

Carol: And you're saying it to?

Amy: Well, all that comes into my mind is when I'd been naughty, he'd tell me to go up to my room and take my knickers off and wait for Daddy. [*Amy at this point blushed crimson, and picked up her handbag as if to leave, about ten minutes before the end of the session.*]

The challenge for Carol was whether she should try to elicit more of what was probably a traumatic story Amy seemed to have recalled, the telling of which was in itself a form of awakening or satori. It seemed highly likely that the story would not be 'nice', in the way Amy liked life to be. With two more sessions of therapy available, Carol decided instead to concentrate on doing what she could to persuade Amy to return next week.

Carol: You look agitated, and I remember how a trainer I had used to say 'There's no learning without churning'. What seems to me important is that you have discovered how some childhood fear has been the root of your stutter. And you have noticed the mechanics of it, as well as the feelings. Let's see if by changing the mechanics, you begin to change the feeling. I'm just interested in whether that happens, I'm not suggesting that it should happen.

Amy: And for singing they tell you how to breathe, so no wonder it was OK. And that was at school.

Carol: [*Notes the implied message that only at school was it easy to drop being afraid. She chooses to persist in these final moments of the session with 'nice' aspects of the difficulty.*] So can you think of something to try out at home that will give you that information?

Amy: I'm not quite sure I'll be able to come next week.

Carol: Amy, you have done an important piece of work this afternoon in unlocking your voice. However that fear, almost panic, started, what is left is a habit of speech that you can probably change. Finding some experiment to practice will help that process.

Amy: [*after a pause*] It seems silly to say I could sing what I say.

Carol: It doesn't sound silly to me.

Amy: If I sort of thought about it as if I was going to sing it, but really said it.

Carol: I think you've begun. You didn't stutter. [*Amy struggles to say something else.*] And that's perhaps how it will be at first. You know how to be different. But until a new habit is established, the old one will keep popping up.

Amy: I'll do what I can to come along next week. And I'll keep doing the homework.

In the following, penultimate session, Amy's score rate on speaking without stuttering had improved considerably. She still stuttered badly if she did not pretend inwardly that she was going to sing her reply.

Carol: It looks as if your body has developed a really strong habit of tensing up and then going into stutter mode. And you've found a way of making a new habit, of controlled breathing and easy speech. We haven't gone much into the other side of it, how that fear and tensing started.

Amy: [*stuttering*] We don't need to do that. [*Composes herself*] I want to thank you very much, it's really been worth it.

Carol: That sounds like a goodbye statement, I'll be sorry if …

Amy: Oh no, I'm sure I'll be along next week.

She did not return, but sent her last cheque and an expensive card with neatly-written warm thanks. Carol suspected that just the mention of 'the other side of it' had driven Amy to leave. In supervision, she decided that she would have felt collusive if she had pretended that she believed it would be enough just to change behaviour, without any finishing of what was unfinished from the time when Amy was aged seven. Her supervisor warned her against rigid thinking.

It seems likely that as a species we communicated and experienced without, or with primitive, speech, for very much longer than with our present sophisticated systems. It seems too that we hold memory in muscle, in our hearing, sight, sense of smell, touch and proprioception. Just as adequate therapy can sometimes be done with only words and feeling, so it can demonstrably be done, as here, with a strong emphasis on sensation and physicality.

A valuable area of experimentation is to do with proprioception, the sense and awareness of the body. Many people will learn a great deal from paying attention to their posture, movement, breathing and patterns of muscular tension, and the ways these vary as circumstances change. When there is enough sense of what has perhaps become a dysfunctional habit, then deliberate changes can be tried out, and the effects on contact and sense of self explored. Finding that it is more pleasant, indeed even possible, to look at people without holding your breath or stiffening the neck or raising the shoulders may be a life-changing discovery.

The ideal or visionary experiment

Some of the most important concerns and emphases in therapy are likely to be to do with hope and aspiration. Plato described the establishing of ideals which by their nature constituted directions and aspirations, though they were unattainable. The vocabulary and conceptualising of what can be seen as our relationship to the present and future has changed through the generations. Religious and spiritual systems are often the formal carriers of this strand of human being. Creative visualising, the transpersonal, are some of the current words conveying some aspects of these perennial needs for hope and awe.

The establishing of range scales at the beginning of BGT is a cautious and somewhat flat-footed form of this kind of experiment. The emphasis here is on the attainable, with timescales stipulated. The 'major and minor goals' experiment goes a little further, in suggesting that every action leads either towards or away from the central aspirations of anyone's life. It is described in Appendix C.

Alongside these, there are many Gestalt so-called fantasy exercises. These involve deliberate imagining, whether of something remembered, or possible in the future, or simply fantastical. Many of them can be seen as having two outcomes. One is the possible direct experience of a free creative state. This process in itself is novel and of importance to many people who try out such an experiment. That is the process outcome. The content of the fantasy is also very often inspirational for the person fantasising. Playing in imagination, perhaps taking on a different form, different attributes and abilities, travelling in time as well as space, without the constraints of physics, can have the effect of lifting the person fantasising into awareness and hopes that are more usually hidden under habits of thought and action. Transpersonal experience is connected to this state (Newberg et al., 2001; Saver and Rabin, 1997).

The bridges between the aware and unaware seem comparatively unguarded in fantasy, in a way that overlaps with light hypnosis. People who object to letting down their guard need to be respected for this. It is true to say that in most cases they will not produce images, even if they say they want to. However, some clear rules of procedure are best kept to by the therapist in these experiments. See Appendix C, and Houston (1998a).

Between-session experiments

In time-limited work, tasks the client wants to try out at home or outside the formal therapy session may enhance his learning very much, as the vignette about Amy illustrates. The sensitive therapist will not hold a rigid expectation that people will do out-of-hours assignments. For some, it is not appropriate.

One very successful eight-session episode involved a woman who had kept quiet about an extraordinary amount of her life. She had kept quiet about her husband's homosexuality, kept quiet about her unfulfilled dreams of living in the countries where she could use her linguistic skills, kept quiet about being cheated of an inheritance, and so on. Letting herself tell, and feel the emotionality of the story of her life, was itself the therapy.

Setting her tasks, perhaps to tell secrets to other people outside the therapy, would probably have been beside the point, or at least premature. She needed to clear her mind and find a new direction now her husband was dead. And she did, without extra-curricular tasks.

For many other people, such extra experiments are welcome. The range of them is enormous. What is stressed here is that they need to be:

1. A development from the therapy tasks. It might be tempting to throw in a different topic to be worked on between sessions. This should generally be resisted. In brief work, a clear gestalt formation needs to be maintained, with the trust that one fractal of a difficulty or a person is likely to influence the whole;
2. A mutual negotiation or a suggestion from the client, not a therapist imposition. The concept of what can be seen as homework has such strong associations for all parties, that there is a risk of it becoming resented and therefore destructive rather than constructive;
3. Clearly understood for their relevance to the client's area of interest;
4. Taken on with respect for the wisdom of behavioural therapy. In other words, if the homework is not done or is oddly done, the therapist does not blame the client, but takes some responsibility for having allowed it to be set up in such a way that it was not attained.

Very often indeed, a between-session task is easily invented on the spot. Perls's analogy of eating and other experience may come strongly to mind, for example, when working with some people. They may find it interesting to try out staying aware of their eating, or concentrating on their chewing, or whatever, at their meals between sessions.

Eager clients who are gobblers may well gobble such an idea, and determine to stay fully aware of every morsel that passes their lips, until it has reached the large intestine. Failure is probably built in to such an ambition. Negotiating to a small enough bite at this experiment can of itself be part of working through the difficulty that presents.

This example is meant as a caution to hasten slowly, and work towards small distinct successes or discoveries, rather than global behaviour change at one fell swoop.

'Here's one I prepared earlier'

Clients are unlikely to spend time considering the material of experiments before they enter therapy, but therapists do have this opportunity. It is worth taking it, and going to workshops or reading books where a range of experiments can be witnessed and learnt, ready for adaptation to a particular group or client. H.G. Rosenthal's recent (2001) book is one offering a wide background knowledge.

Mistake and recovery

In a review such as this of many sensitive and imaginative ways of approaching and working with troubled people, it may be easy for the reader to suppose that this book is written for perfect people, for therapists who move sure-footedly from clearly-negotiated therapeutic goals to unerringly-appropriate interventions, and thus to an unsullied therapeutic relationship and a perfectly-rounded episode of therapy. This is perhaps the Platonic ideal, so, as was said earlier, it is a direction rather than a place likely to be reached entirely.

Therapists have preoccupations that sometimes intrude into their work. They have their own Achilles' heels, touchy areas where they are likely to respond from a neurotic rather than a contemporary and appropriate stance. They misremember and forget. They stay quiet when words are needed, and blurt when they might do better to go on listening. None of this is much to be condoned. But it is part of what at times happens, and so deserves some attention in the context of BGT.

Focal length

An antidote to the harm that can follow a therapist's mistakes is for her to cultivate a habit of moving mentally between close and wide focus. With Amy, close focus was needed to observe how she preserved her stutter physically. Wide focus was needed, for instance, to make a very rapid and silent choice between pursuing what seemed likely to be the emotional origins of her stutter, or putting a higher priority on making it easy for her to return to the next session.

A supervisee reported this sequence:

> A young woman BGT client referred within a doctor's practice was suffering various physical symptoms in her genital area, and had come to him complaining of not wanting sex. The therapist experienced her as flirtatious, and noticed his own unacknowledged reciprocal feelings. In her third session, she said, 'I didn't like it at all when you talked about your cup running over into mine. That felt a very invasive image'. He was taping the session, and knew he had not said this. He told her what he had said: in response to her report of some good news, in the context of a church choir practice, he had said that it sounded as if at last her cup was running over. She insisted on her version, and challenged him to re-play the tape. He felt protective, not wanting to shame her, so said that was not necessary.

In the calm of a supervision session, he saw that his own sexual feelings had made him be chivalrous rather than straightforward. 'She's done it before,' he said, 'telling me I said things I didn't say'. He came to see that letting her re-play the tape would have dealt with something potentially important: his client needed to know that she projected her invasive feelings so thoroughly that she became sure the other person was saying what was not said.

By the end of the supervision he had also come to see that his immediate denial of her accusation was in his eyes another mistake, this time to do with childhood memories of his own, of being misheard and wrongly accused. He concluded that there would have been more therapeutic potential in finding out about her feelings towards him on hearing such a statement, before, if need be, demonstrating the facts.

The beam in his own eye, to pursue the Biblical imagery, was that until this session he had not admitted to himself his sexual response to the client. He cringed at the rather giggly conversation on his tape. The following week's tape contained this sequence:

> *Client*: I hope you're not going to say any more naughty things this week and upset me like last time.
> *Therapist*: [*close focus*] You think I'm naughty?
> *Client*: There! You've just said you are.
> *Therapist*: [*close focus*] You're smiling and have some extra colour in your face. I'm interested in what you're imagining about me as a naughty therapist.
> *Client*: Well, there's certainly plenty in the papers every Sunday! I'm not going to say!
> *Therapist*: [*After pause, during which he did not smile in response to her arch looks. Wide focus*] What I'm remembering now is what you've told me about you and your father. And I guess that if I responded as he did, that would be a great deal worse than naughty, it would be irresponsible. So here we are with a very important moment, when you are being as charming and flirtatious as you can be, to a man who is out of bounds; we are going to discover what happens to your feelings when the other person stays out of bounds.
> *Client*: Oh, you are being really boring this morning.

Therapist: [*close focus*] The first thing that happens is that you return to the battle, the Cupid's battle. [*She looks down and pouts. He waits, and she begins to cry. There is more interchange.*]
Client: [*near the end of the session*] This is the only way I know how to be with men.
Therapist: [*close focus*] What? Like this, telling your experience truthfully?
Client: I meant being flirty, even with – anyone. Otherwise I'll be nothing.
Therapist: You don't seem at all flirty at this moment.
Client: And I'm not nothing, you're right. But I'm very uncomfortable.
Therapist: [*wide focus*] We're almost at time. My impression is that you have done a lot of work today, and brought out into the open some of the fears that go with this very successful, very charming way you can use when you are with men. I'm not surprised that you feel uncomfortable. I think of a hermit crab growing out of one shell, and having to be quite exposed while it looks for another that fits it better.
Client: Two more sessions. Do you think I'll make it? If you've got a moment or two longer now maybe we …
Therapist: It's time. Let's talk about it next Wednesday.

The therapist was pleased with himself when he played this tape in supervision. He was convinced that as he removed himself from the erotic level of their dialogue, he on the one hand helped the client do the same, and on the other, was more in touch with what he called his fatherly tenderness towards her. He saw the attempted extension of the session as an important test for both of them of his ability to hold all the therapeutic boundaries. He saw that at times it is the work of the client to show her ways of trying to break boundaries. It is the work of the BGT therapist to resist every such attempt.

Summation

The middle phase of BGT will vary markedly between person and person, and be closely connected to the earlier, possibly partly-revised, assessment phase. From the therapist's standpoint, the theory of paradoxical change underpins the work, and attention needs to be given also to other influences towards change that are less theoretically explicit.

Practice points

Experimentation can usefully be seen in categories, in all of which the assimilation or talking through that follows may to advantage be systemised as described here.

While keeping time in the foreground, the BGT therapist is careful to hurry slowly, to take time to expose process and work through her own perceived mistakes. She will be alert to the occasional rare moment of transformative experience that may turn out to be the fulcrum of insight and change.

6

The Ending

T.S. Eliot's line, 'In my end is my beginning' (1944: 23), has a resonance for all therapy. In brief therapy more than elsewhere, the converse also has great importance. In our beginning is our end. Janice Scott and Glenys Jacques in their articles on BGT (both 1999) lay proper emphasis on this context of time, that needs frequent acknowledgement in groups or individual work.

A little like the Russian dolls that lend themselves so conveniently to such analogies, BGT can be seen as a nest of gestalt formations. Within each session gestalts will form, and at best will be completed. Then, each session can usefully be seen as having the form of a gestalt (Nevis, 1987). Some overall topic or direction will likely emerge and then achieve some sort of resolution. Any tasks done between sessions can in part be looked at as the opening of a new gestalt, or a rounding-off of one begun in the session.

The outer layer of the doll is the whole episode of therapy, the five, six, ten or more sessions that are allotted or decided on. The inner layers are the particular aspects of the client's experience that are discovered or reported and worked on in each session. Some such image needs to be at the back of the therapist's mind, helping her quietly organise the experience of the therapy for all parties to it. It will almost certainly be there too in the minds of group members or clients, whether in awareness or out of it. Time is one of the omnipresent field conditions through which humans seem to organise their experience.

Half full or half empty?

Perception of time is highly idiosyncratic. It is frequently confused with will or energy. An interviewer on election night after a low poll asked someone if he had voted. 'No, I didn't have time.' 'But it is seven thirty in the evening, the polls are open till ten and the polling booth is across the road there, and you are sitting in a pub garden drinking beer.'

This incident can be contrasted with Brian Keenan's description of one moment in his monotonous incarceration in Beirut:

> With calm, disinterested deliberation I pull from my head the filthy towel that blinds me, and slowly turn to go like a dog well-trained to its corner, to sit

> again, and wait and wait, forever waiting. I look at this food I know to be the same as it always has been.
>
> But wait. My eyes are almost burned by what I see. There's a bowl in front of me that wasn't there before. A brown button bowl and in it some apricots, some small oranges, some nuts, cherries, a banana. The fruits, the colours, mesmerise me in a quiet rapture that spins through my head. I am entranced by colour. I lift an orange into the flat filthy palm of my hand and feel and smell and lick it. (1993: 68)

Moments such as this give a sense of expansion of the psyche, even a glimpse of the continuum between time and space. They seem to transcend time, in the largeness and intensity of what is apprehended in an overflowing instant. Because this quality of experience is not much spoken of in psychotherapy texts, I come back to it in several parts of this book. The purpose of many spiritual practices appears to be the development of a readiness to be so fully present that such experiences will happen. To my mind it is a pity that any division is made between full perception and ordinary life. The evidence is that most people know such moments. And for most of us they are rare. Good therapy, in other words, an attitude of openness and compassion and honesty, probably expands the possibility that such life-filled and life-filling instants will occur for the client.

Part of the work of the therapist is to keep time, and the ending implicit in it, appropriately in her and the client's or group's awareness. At a simple level, with people who move easily into the illusion of timelessness, the therapist may find it politic to comment that only so many sessions are left. With others, who seem overwhelmed by what they see as their own slowness, the therapist does better to comment that there are still two, or however many, sessions to go. In few areas are those empathic processes, now partly attributed to mirror neurons (Gallese and Goldman, 1998), more delicately important in BGT than in this appreciation of the meanings that clients give to time, and the relation to it that ensues.

Endings, catastrophe and hope

A supervisee accepted into BGT a young man whose mother had died when he was 23 months old. The supervisor felt deeply uneasy about this, worried that the brief therapy would be a painful re-evocation of that first short period of attention, concern and warmth, to be followed by the equivalent of sudden death. This young man's presenting difficulty was to do with sustaining relationships. He walked out on friends and lovers, and then 'could not be bothered' to re-engage with them.

The focus of the therapy then became an aware experiment in how the client might perceive this ending in the same way as that first tragic one with his mother, and how he might perceive it differently. The early pattern was acknowledged and respected. The present difference was elicited and assimilated. Follow-up phone calls and three further sessions at longer intervals were agreed by the funding agency, and served to consolidate the client's new learning that he could keep hope, could in a sense keep another person alive, after he had stopped seeing them.

Many people who come into BGT, indeed into any therapy, have very strong emotions about ending. These feelings may be so uncomfortable that they are masked, and either not perceived by the client, or are translated into confusing behaviour. So our young man in this example walked out on people who presumably, even if told the origins of his behaviour, would sense it as both hurtful and illogical. Why do to others what has hurt you so much?

We need to be alert to hints about the client's attitudes to ending. Some people will choose brief therapy because it seems to let them off the threat of too much intimacy. Their major solution to relational difficulties may be to run for the door. Extreme co-operation, gratefulness, good cheer and good manners are sometimes a clue to this stance. The well-brought-up child behaves as his parents or mentors demand, but only for so long, before retreating to the depression that substitutes for open conflict with others. BGT is possible with such people, so long as the therapist is not gulled by the charm of what seems a really willing client. At best, she will see the possibility that the phoney layer, the persona, is often very like the true self. The persona just tries too hard, and in consequence often tires or jangles himself and others.

This is not just about a distinct phase of BGT called 'dealing with the ending'. It is doubtful if there often needs to be such a thing. It seems as if most of us, as I say, carry some unconscious stopwatch that helps shape events and relationships, and give them meaning. Psychoanalytic psychotherapists, who lay great emphasis on transference, recognise that in brief therapy people are unlikely to develop heavy transferential feelings.

In Gestalt terms, the organism generally likes to put a pint, not a quart, in a pint pot. Both or all parties to the work will sense differences in themselves and their perceptions, as the large gestalt moves to conclusion. Anticipated relief may cheer up a low-key interaction. Sadness will be felt a little or more if trust and openness have been established, and the end draws nigh. If the phenomenology is let into the dialogue, there will at best be self-regulation of the ending. As in a concerto, the themes will be heard again in resolved form, the pace will change in a way appropriate to what has been before, and move towards quiet or to a final crescendo.

Reminders for the trainee therapist

Less-experienced practitioners can usefully contrast the following pieces of advice about making a closure in open-ended work, with what is needed in BGT.

The ideal ending, perhaps, is one negotiated between patient and therapist.

If this is an ideal, it is not available in BGT, where the ending is dictated by the form of therapy. The learning that comes from dealing with uncertainty is thus reduced. The comfort that comes from the great anxiety-reducer – structure – is substituted.

The manner of ending probably has bearing on the troubles the patient first brought to the therapist.

This holds true in BGT, and will be talked of more later in this chapter.

The client can only do one of two things. She can make this ending in the way she is used to in other parts of her life; or she can make a new kind of ending.

It is worth raising awareness about which of these seems to be happening. Then you can both look at what works or is advantageous about this way, and/or, what does not work and makes for more potential distress, and for whom.

Endings mostly involve some kind of loss, and consequent grieving and adjustment to change. They mostly involve some advantages too. These include gains in learning, and there may be relief of many other kinds.

In therapy, this relief might simply be the freeing of time and income, for example, as a result of ending therapy. If only one polarity of ending is explored, the therapist has not done all her work. In BGT, however, some clients will probably be helped by some discussion and planning of the future. In the extreme constraint of very brief work, with some people at some times, the following adage may therefore be more relevant than a high focus on the nature of the present ending.

Ending makes space for a new beginning.

In brief work, this truth is of special importance. More often than some advocates of long-term therapy acknowledge, BGT can bring about a large shift of perception. What it cannot do is give a supported lengthy period of working through or assimilation.

A behaviour that has been created and honed over 10 or 30 years may suddenly be understood as irrelevant and destructive in the present. Experiments in new behaviours may be undertaken successfully and appreciated. But there are some well-worn neural pathways leading to the old behaviour. Without monitoring and encouragement, the client may have difficulty in keeping the new pathways open sufficiently often for them to become well-established and easily accessible.

An important part of many episodes of BGT therefore includes talking through tactics and strategy for the client to pursue, after the formal therapy has ended. For some people, asking friends, relatives or colleagues to monitor some new practice, or comment on lapses from it, may make for more general as well as this specific social support. The socially timorous may decide to set up a programme of theatre or cinema or restaurant visits each week, to which they invite others. People who spend more time in contact than withdrawal may find that keeping a diary helps them monitor their own progress.

Many other experiments can be sketched out by the client, with the therapist's co-operation, as enhancements of life after therapy, and consolidation of what has been glimpsed or briefly experienced. At least one follow-up session, to happen after four to twelve weeks, has many uses. One of them is to hold the focus on the client's continuing engagement with what has gone on in the small cluster of meetings.

The resource or tool box

For some people, it will have become clear during the work, if it was not at the beginning, that more formal therapy as soon as possible is advisable. Here the therapist needs what in another place (Houston, 1995: 22–3) I have called a resource box. This is a file of contacts and references. Practitioners of BGT do well to keep an updated file of people and places, groups, practitioners, drop-in centres, day hospitals and what all else that may make a speedy path from BGT to a further intervention, if one cannot be made through internal channels. At the time of writing, GAUK (the Gestalt Association of the United Kingdom) is installing some relevant material on its website. This will be an aid, but cannot replace the particular local knowledge useful to each BGT practitioner.

Stopping or ending

A distinction between ending, bringing to a conclusion, and stopping – here meaning sudden abandonment – is useful in this context. The word 'bolters' might have served as a heading here. This somewhat frivolous term is from Nancy Mitford's novels, in which the protagonist's mother was recognised by her family as a serial eloper. 'Stoppers' seems more adequate, if the word is used to suggest truncation, rather than completion.

Not infrequently, people stop therapy rather than making an acknowledged end in the way so far described in this chapter. If your client gives clues about being a bolter or hider, someone whose solution to problems or difficulties is to keep out of sight of them, you may be of use if you talk to her, as soon as this pattern emerges, about her possible disappearance from the therapy, and about what she would like you to do should that happen. Her reply will tell you a great deal about how to work with her in general. It is very common for the pattern to be made very clear within the first session.

Some people who come to brief therapy have, from a great variety of field conditions, become habitual truncaters. This may well emerge when they tell something of their life, or just their previous history of therapy. One man may report that he was forced to leave a number of therapists who were deeply unsatisfactory in one way or another. It is possible that someone is unfortunate enough to engage with several unsatisfactory therapists one after another. But the possibility will probably also occur to the BGT therapist that the client's attitude rather than the therapists' competence might have been of significance here.

Another person may be hazy about his reasons for stopping seeing previous therapists after very short intervals, and forgetful too about what communication happened between therapist and client on those occasions. Someone else, who has not been in therapy before, may tell of many job, location and partner changes, in a way that alerts the therapist to the possibility that extremely brief therapy is threatened here.

In the constraints of a medical practice, BGT therapists supervised by the writer sometimes guess accurately that they are seeing a stopper, and resort to dealing with each session as if it might be the last. This decision is usually to do with recognition of the apparently impoverished resources of the client, who may combine low educational attainment, large social problems in family, debt and illegal activity, and confused or frightened contact style. In an ideal world, such a person might be offered more substantial help than six or eight sessions of talking therapy. In a mean world, the therapist might improve her success figures by not accepting such a person into BGT at all.

> People I supervise not infrequently take on such clients, often using the one or three sessions they actually turn out to have, for diagnosis, challenging, and referring on. Sometimes their prognostication is wrong, and the client stays the course. That is often to do with the therapist's skill in engaging someone not used to engagement. But that cannot be counted on, so the supervisory question that seems especially useful is: 'What are you going to regret not having done or said if X does not come back after this session?' In other words, the therapist needs to be encouraged to use her best powers, to make the fullest therapeutic contact that is feasible. 'Putting on hold', 'thinking about', 'keeping at the back of the mind', are delaying notions that have less place with stoppers than they may with other people.

When a client stops coming unexpectedly, you need generally to get in touch, to say if you are still expecting her. The task is to do all you can to avoid either shaming or colluding. Supervision should be of help here, if necessary, in helping you to keep a dialogic stance with someone who stays out of touch. Experience teaches that a second follow-up note is not infrequently followed by a return to therapy, sometimes much later.

Pre-emption

With other people who have a history of truncating, pre-emption can be fruitful. This extract is from a first session of BGT:

> *Client*: Yes, I've seen seven or eight therapists and people over the years.
> *Therapist*: [*Sensing dismissiveness in the client's phrase.*] How did these encounters end?
> *Client*: Well, they got my back up. I know I'm thin-skinned, but they'd do something and I'd think 'Well, that's it then', so that would be the end.
> *Therapist*: Did you manage to talk this through with any of them?
> *Client*: Not really. Well, you can't if you aren't there, can you?
> *Therapist*: My guess is that one day or another I might do something, the way these other people did.
> *Client*: No, you seem fine.
> *Therapist*: On half an hour's acquaintance, maybe. What's interesting me is whether you want to risk ending the same way with me.
> *Client*: No, I'm sure it'll be all right.
> *Therapist*: [*persisting and friendly*] I want to play with the idea that somehow or other I put my foot in it with you, say something that puts your back up. Then it seems as if that's the end, unless we can make some alternative plan.
> *Client*: The trouble is I get hurt, and stay away, and then by the time I feel better, weeks have passed and I'm embarrassed to go back.
> *Therapist*: Yes, I see. So you did want to go back? [*The client nods.*] So, just say we get to such a moment. Can you think of anything we could do differently?
> *Client*: I just ought to be more adult, I suppose.
> *Therapist*: I'm talking about feasibility, not moral positions. What emergency strategy can we cook up?
> *Client*: Well, it sounds feeble but if you could email me or something a bit friendly if I didn't show. [*Laughs embarrassedly*] Just to show you care.

It is not difficult to make some accurate guesses about the sort of deficits in parenting this client had received in childhood. In the event, the emergency strategy was never needed. However, the client said that knowing that he was not going to be abandoned made his whole approach to this episode of therapy more trusting than he had been with any other therapist.

For the sake of brevity, this example is quoted. Others need a more elaborate contract. In any such negotiation, the challenge for the BGT worker is to distinguish between what Perls calls spoilt brats, and people like this willing client who confesses a dysfunctional behaviour he wants to buck. The unkindly-termed spoilt brat is more likely to suggest telephone access, extra sessions, freedom to come and go, and many other devices that are more to do with plaguing the other than with being co-operative. Within the confines of brief therapy, there is unlikely to be space enough to explore the aetiology and self-punitive aspects of such behaviour via an acting-out route.

Considerable skill is needed with such a person, to hold the therapeutic boundaries, and at the same time maximise therapeutic impact. The following vignette from another assessment session illustrates some of what I describe. This client described her difficulty in maintaining relationships. The therapist again asked what the two of them might devise if this difficulty surfaced in the therapy.

Client: Well, I see it as your job really. I mean you are the counsellor. I think you're meant to be good at relationships.

Therapist: And what does my job entail at that point, when you've walked out in the way you describe?

Client: [*with satisfaction*] You'd've had it then, wouldn't you? Nothing you could do then!

Therapist: Thank you. That's a gift.

Client: Are you being sarky?

Therapist: No. I'll tell you what went on. For a moment I felt almost physically winded. Then I jumped to imagining that you showed me just now a whole cameo of power, and being overpowered, and the pain around that. I imagined you being ignored or walked out on, and then you starting to do the same to other people.

Client: That doesn't ring any bells for me. [*Pause*]

Therapist: [*in a friendly tone, slowly*] One of my interests is in doing what I can to allow your power in our work together. So after this meeting I'll ask you to have a night's sleep before you ring the surgery to say whether you'd like to continue. The work needs to be on your terms. And I guess from what you've said that the tussle for you may be between, on the one hand, somehow paying me out, paying out all the people who have let you down, by disappearing; on the other hand, there's coming back and seeing how together we can have a first go at cracking what's become a big enough problem for you to want to seek help.

In supervision the counsellor reported that she noticed a moment of rage when the client said it was the counsellor's job to take care of the relationship, and again at the 'Doesn't ring any bells'. Luckily, instead of contesting, she used a kind of martial arts strategy and did not resist. When the client gloated at the thought of walking out, the counsellor felt confident of her diagnosis, and with a renewed sense of competence, was able to go on talking from an empathic rather than a defensive stance.

This client did not telephone as asked, or reappear, until eight months later. She then asked to see the same counsellor, and in this second meeting said she had kept thinking about 'paying people out', and had realised that she felt angry most of the time. From this new beginning, a six-session piece of work was completed, and the client said she had changed and was making friends at work.

This incident is a rare example of evidence of the usefulness of engaging courageously with a client who is showing her symptom, rather than showing her determination to change. It takes faith to believe that both aspects are present, when only one is manifest.

Reviewing the evidence

The range scales that the client filled in at the beginning of therapy need to have been consulted from time to time. The last session is the moment when the client can look to see if he has moved towards the goals he first described, and by how much. Doing this near the beginning of the last session will for many clients lead to a useful conversation about the future. If progress has outstripped the goals, it may be worthwhile to talk about what seems to have led to this discrepancy. Does the client have a generally gloomy view of how well he can do? Is he pleased with where he is? Does he feel nervous and self-doubting? Such questions are part of the assimilation of learning, and preparation for possible setbacks when the therapist is no longer part of the scene.

It is just as useful to talk carefully through underachievement on the original goals. Were the goals unrealistic? What are the client's feelings towards himself as he sees this datum? How does the underachievement affect the client's hopes and fears about the future? What are his feelings towards the therapist in the light of this apparent underachievement?

The answers to all these questions and the others provoked by each client, can be related back to the difficulty that brought that person to therapy. Any improved coping can be commented on, and a strategy for maintenance talked through as in the following vignette from a final (fifth) session with a 28-year-old depressed client:

Client: [*looking at scales*] I'd forgotten I'd said I'd be back at work by the time we'd finished. I'm not, am I?

Therapist: You told me your company has just gone into liquidation.

Client: That's upset me, not hitting my target. I feel I've failed myself somehow.

Therapist: I'm remembering the perfectionism you've often talked about here. And that list we made of the ways you can make your depression worse.

Client: [*smiling*] Oh God, I'm supposed to look on the bright side. Well, I've moved out of my parents' place and I've booked a walking holiday, and I must say I'm pleased about both of those.

Therapist: I feel my own perfectionism coming up. I felt dubious at the time about it being feasible to find a job in five weeks, so I reckon I should have questioned you more about it at the beginning.

Client: You did. I remember.

Therapist: So perhaps we're back with one of your self-sabotage devices. Set a high target, don't get there, feel gloomy.

Client: It works like a charm. [*Pause*]

Therapist: It sounds to me more like a spell, a bad spell, not a charm.

Client: And now it's a case of 'Can I produce a stronger spell to get rid of that one?'

Therapist: What do you reckon? [*By this stage, the therapist trusts the self-support capacity of the client.*]

Client: I need to remind myself, somehow, before I slither down into the pit again.

Therapist: I'm remembering what Fritz Perls said about getting a little Fritzy doll. That was meant to be a reminder. [*Two minutes passed. With some effort, the client then managed to ask for a stone from a bowl of shells and pebbles in the consulting room.*]

Client: Only to borrow. I could bring it back when we have that session in a month.

Therapist: Do you know yet how you'll use it?

Client: I'll keep it in my left-hand pocket, and feel it solid and warm in my hand whenever I need to.

The client has made an experiment. He has invented a way to reassure or encourage himself.

Completion of cycle

One simple way of auditing the last session or so of the group or one-to-one therapy, is to look at what has gone on in terms of the 'cycle of experience'. What are the gestalts that can be seen as fully experienced, assimilated, learned from and laid to rest? What others are still in some way incomplete? What needs to be done about these?

In a group, people may want to work in pairs to recall all this to the present. They may be invited to see if they can find ways of doing some of the finishing off that comes into the foreground. 'Finishing off' in this sense may mean the taking of some action, rather than making a full completion. Someone in mourning may, for example, still be aware of some denial of the reality of the recent death. Acknowledging that she does feel and know the loss, as well as having other moments when she does not, may be a sufficient reminder to her that the progress of grief is not often smooth or short.

Someone who is still in dread that he will respond to what has been called his low violence threshold, and lash out impulsively, may do well to enact one more short reminder of how he has learned in the therapy to do otherwise.

The learnings in BGT are often new and still far from being an easy habit, by the time that goodbyes are said. In this context, it is a very good idea to have people spell out what sort of social support they need and can access from now on. In a group, other members may become part of this system, to mutual advantage. In a pair, the knowledge from the therapist's resource box may be needed, for someone who has few friends or an unsupportive family.

Marking the end

In the bustle of checking range scales, doing last experiments and making plans, the reality of the end itself may be glossed over. In a group, there is scope for inviting the invention of some ceremony to mark the end of a final session.

Many years ago, I co-led an 11-session group on television. By the last session, all of us had grown accustomed to the demands and implicit rules of the television studio. At a certain point in the recording, which was to be edited down later, one of the group members said that he felt we had finished. We had said and done what we needed. Others agreed. Calmly and without any premeditation, we all got up and walked quietly off the set, a most taboo act, but one which turned out to make an excellent visual end to the series. I quote that here, to encourage trust in the group, that multi-bodied organism through which much wisdom can be evinced.

That ending was not awarely planned. Many others in my experience have been invented on the spot, to express what in that group at that time needs to be expressed. Standing in a circle and looking at each other, then turning and looking outwards, or standing with shut eyes and with the sense of having the group behind us, in more than one sense, are two examples I remember.

In a society of less and less formality, finding a rite to mark an ending may be to give the opportunity for a last moment of full contact, of final contact.

Practice points

At the first session, the therapist will do well to be alert to patterns of aborted endings reported by the client. If these are talked out, the chances of changing the pattern are increased.

The reality of the present ending is also worth acknowledging. How it connects to the issue the client brought to therapy, and how it connects to other endings in the client's life, may well be noticed.

In a group particularly, some brief ritual to mark the end is a way of giving reality and value to it.

The end may have been in mind since the beginning of BGT. More than in an extended therapy, the end in BGT is likely to mark new beginnings, perhaps in terms of new activities or further therapeutic work for the client. These can be planned with the therapist, in the light of a last look perhaps at any range scales that have been set up.

7

A BGT Individual Case Study

Here I will describe one individual five-plus-one episode, chosen both because it could be seen as having some success, and to show that something can on occasion be achieved in what turns out to be very brief contact. Exhaustive cover of any of this material is impossible within one book. The aim is to pick out illustrations of Brief Gestalt method, both where it can be seen to work, and where some aspects of it are more problematic.

The reader will inevitably have even less data to work from than does the therapist. But the therapists too in brief intervention may, by the standards of some therapeutic methods, be quite underinformed.

Before seeing Susan, Derek, a young-looking 40-year-old BG Therapist in Primary Health Care was simply given her name. He came to supervision after his first session with Susan, and handed over a supervision memorandum sheet (see facing page).

Derek was very glum about his apparent ineffectiveness with Susan. He had seen her at the end of the day and he was tired. He suspected he had been slightly terse in eliciting her constructs to work on. These were: (a) to close down her business honourably; and (b) not to have a breakdown.

Susan put X as her present position, Y as where she would like to be by the end of the therapy, and Z as her final position on the first of the two constructs.

0	1	2	3	4	5X	6	7Y	8Z	9

She was persuaded not to put 9 as her final ambition on this scale, and her perfectionism was noted by Derek.

On the second construct, 'not having a breakdown', she marked her scale:

0	1	2Z	3	4Y	5	6	7	8X	9

She agreed to have her husband and a friend who lived near to fill in observer ratings on similar charts. These would not show forecasts, like hers, but their sense of where she was now, at the time she finished her six sessions, and at the time of the follow-up.

Client: Susan	**Therapist**: Derek
Referred by: Dr Harrison	**Date of first session**: 6 March 2002
Time contract:	Five sessions and follow-up offered.
Presenting difficulty:	Fear of breakdown while closing down Italian villa holiday business, because husband has developed MS.
Risk:	12 years ago had breakdown and was in nursing home for four months.
Medication:	Refuses any.
Client's hope of therapy:	To avoid breakdown and close business honourably.
Therapist's first impressions:	Very taut lady. Very neat. Talks past therapist. He feels powerless.

Derek: I feel I'm more or less in nonsense land, accepting a negative definition like that. But she wouldn't put it any other way.
Supervisor: Interestingly, the scale is positive.
Derek: Now you spell it out, yes, I can see it now. A bit of parallel process there, of getting stuck in her dread of doing badly.
Supervisor: You look more alive now. That's after I trusted your good judgement. How much are you trusting hers?
Derek: Not enough. She seems disapproving of me, and I feel disapproving of her. I'm not pleased with myself.

He felt he had done badly by commenting how often she spoke of not wanting to collapse or break down. In response he had attempted a trial dose of a Gestalt intervention, and wondered aloud how she would sound to herself if she said the opposite, that she would like to collapse. Her acerbity in dealing with this made him suspect that he had been too close for comfort, and that she unawarely perhaps yearned for escape via what she called breakdown.

He agreed with his supervisor that Susan was someone who might be slow to form much trust. The bedrock of a strong therapeutic relationship, in which confrontation might be welcomed, would probably be slow to occur.

She had earlier in her life been a headmistress, and he said that for much of the interview he felt like a very disappointing pupil being given a wigging. He supposed that this admonitory manner was about all Susan could find at the moment to keep herself going. In terms of interruption to contact as a diagnostic measure (Philippson, 1999), angry deflection was a strong part of her style. She also spoke a great deal of her horror of letting people down. Derek noted that he kept getting a dismayed guilty feeling that he was letting her down. When he said so, she pursed her lips and drew her feet back, though she did not reply directly.

In conversation with his supervisor, Derek became more aware of the mismatch between him with his youthful looks, and Susan's authoritarian manner and older years. As there was no other counsellor attached to the Health Centre, he was not in a position to refer her on. (This example has been chosen partly as an acknowledgement of the less than ideal conditions in which much BGT is conducted.)

Derek's feeling response was to want to get to the heart of what he saw as Susan's troubles. At her age, this exit from a business might turn out to be retirement, and retirement in order to tend a progressively less able husband. It was understandable that her whole sense of herself was involved in making a good end to her business, and doing well by the clients of nearly a dozen years. But the future implications of retirement were not what she had come to see him about, and he must not impose them on her, he decided. Instead, he resolved to accept the surface problem as she stated it, and concentrate on whatever she meant by 'breakdown avoidance'.

This temptation is one that is frequent in brief work. There will often be a tension between accepting the client's version, and noticing a larger or different configuration. When to accept the client's version, and when to negotiate about it, is a subtle decision in the assessment session.

Derek put as his likely strategy in the next session to: (a) confront firmly the difficulty of being a younger man in the role of therapist, and give Susan a clear invitation about leaving or staying; and (b) find ways with her of supporting her through the few weeks of their work together, and leaving her with strategies of her own for doing whatever for her was the opposite of collapsing or breaking down.

To this the supervisor added a reminder of Havens's (1986: 53) comment on **complex empathy**, the idea that certain troubled people will recoil at simple empathic statements, but feel met and supported by what others might experience as challenging or even sarcastic.

Second session

Susan arrived early.

Susan: Well, what have you decided to do with me?

Derek: As soon as you asked that, I remembered how you told me you have refused all the medication Dr Harrison has offered.

Susan: This is my last chance, Mr ... Derek.

Derek: You know, I did not feel at ease calling you Susan. Now you say Mister. I think I shall call you Mrs Evans unless you object.

Susan: I'm always Mrs Evans to my clients. There's more trouble this morning from Italy, the owners I told you about last week …

Derek: I want to go back to those words, 'this is my last chance'. They still echo for me.

Susan: I told you, I cannot afford to collapse, I mustn't.

Derek: That is very clear in my mind as your real worry. And you sit very straight and smile at me, and I think of that saying about bending with the wind or breaking.

Susan: Well, I can't afford to let go. Someone has to stand on her two little legs.

Derek: You sound … How old do you sound to yourself as you say 'on her two little legs'?

Susan: It's just a figure of speech.

Derek: Yes, and I notice it as the one you chose. I imagined a small brave child in some scene I don't know about.

Susan: Well, my mother was not a coper. She was a weak person. And my father was not reliable. Not abuse or beating or anything, just not there and no money and she couldn't take it, you see.

Derek: So someone had to keep standing on her two little legs. It's a picture that makes me feel sad.

Susan: Worse troubles than that at sea.

Derek: Mrs Evans, you are facing awful troubles now, and you have told them to me. And I get a strong impression that you are struggling between taking help of any kind, especially perhaps from a younger man, and standing on your own two legs. With parents you could not rely on, I imagine the need to be the coper.

Susan: [*after a long pause*] If you'll tell me what to do, I'll try to do it.

Derek: What I shall ask may sound odd. But it may help us get a better sense of what is going on for you. Let's stand up. [*He does so and she follows uneasily*.] Now just report to me where you feel what in your body. For instance, I notice that my back is more relaxed round the waist area now that I'm on my feet.

Susan: I don't know what I'm supposed to tell you. [*Rather than comment on the resistance, Derek decides to frustrate her deflection by continuing*.]

Derek: Shoulders?

Susan: They are a bit square I suppose.

Derek: [*imitating her stance*] Squaring up? And your legs?

Susan: Braced.

Derek: Now, so far as you can manage, really notice the effect on you of just those things you've reported.

Susan: I feel very rigid. And slightly dizzy. I think I'll sit down. *[She does so and he follows, both noting and allowing her dominance (Mercier and Johnson, 1984).]*

Derek: You are breathing very shallowly.

Susan: Could that be making me dizzy?

Derek: You've made that connection. So you could try one of these. … Oh, you've done what I was going to suggest, a reversal. You just gave a huge sigh.

Susan: Did I? I don't think so.

Soon Susan had agreed with interest to have a video recording of part of the session, via a fixed unmanned camera in the room. It was made clear that she could wipe it after playback, which happened when Derek had noticed a couple of clear examples of her near hyper-ventilation, followed by sighs. This finding intrigued her, and she asked advice about changing.

Derek managed to convert this demand into a counter-demand for her to experiment with something she could invent on the spot. She experimented uncertainly with her breathing, coughing a good deal. Derek helped her and between them they devised a routine of deliberate deeper breathing for extremely short, but increasing-length periods, every day before their next meeting.

Conclusion

Derek found this session hard. Susan seemed to bat him off at least twice for every time she seemed to allow an approach. He was tempted at times to be impatient, at others to fall in with her demand that he be schoolteacher, and at others to give up in the face of what he felt to be her frequent suspicion and hostility.

He believed that he would be of most use if he became neither childish nor bullyingly parental in the ways she subtly demanded. Instead, he remembered Sullivan's counter-assumptive and counter-projective statements (Havens, 1986: 125). He saw these as another description of Gestalt shock or paradox, or crossed transaction, as proper therapeutic frustrations.

Third session

Mrs Evans did not arrive, nor leave any message. Derek was tempted to use the time to have a coffee, make some phone calls and finish notes. He decided instead to sit quietly and learn as best he could from his experience of this phase of the dialogue between him and his client.

He first felt some half-guilty unease. Had he done wrong somehow, and frightened her off? Should he have explored how they named each other, rather than leading on calling her by her formal name? Was the video too intrusive? Blame came next. A professional woman should have had the courtesy to say if she couldn't come. More unease. Perhaps she was stuck in a train, or ill, run over, or dead.

Derek managed to stand back from this obsessing, and imagine what part he might be playing in what system. Perhaps he was being as tautly anxious as Mrs Evans usually seemed. Certainly, she was being unexpectedly let down in her life, both by her husband's illness, and her business, just as she was in a sense letting him down now. He played with ideas of what he needed now, and what she might therefore need. The parental shriek, 'After all I've done for that child!' flashed through his mind, and he recognised his unexpectedly exaggerated need for recognition, in this dialogue. Maybe that was large in her too, and he was going through a parallel process (Hawkins and Shohet, 2000) to hers?

She valued the good opinion of her clients, and that would soon be shaken. The husband sounded somewhat self-centred. How much recognition was Derek giving her? He resolved to give more, and set about writing a note to her:

> Dear Mrs Evans,
>
> I was sorry not to see you today, and hope that you are well and able to come to our next meeting on Tuesday the 15th at the same time.
>
> I hope too that the homework task you devised is being useful to you. It looked to me as if you found an excellent exercise for yourself.
>
> Looking forward very much to seeing you,
>
> Derek Marcham

Headed writing paper gave her the information she would need to get in touch with him, so he forbore asking her to do so.

Session four

To Derek's consternation, Susan did not appear or leave word. He wrote another note:

> Dear Mrs Evans,
>
> I felt concerned when you did not come to our meeting today, fearing that something grave might have prevented you. I do hope that this is not so, and that we shall meet again on the 22nd.
>
> If you have to defer meeting again, would you be kind enough to tell the reception staff, so we can make a later time for you? If something has happened to stop you coming altogether, I would be grateful to know, so that the appointment can be offered to someone else.
>
> Hoping very much that we shall meet next week,
>
> With best wishes,
>
> Derek Marcham

In supervision, Derek realised how cross he felt with Mrs Evans, and how he worried about her.

His supervisor helped him review aloud his misgivings about his attitude to Susan Evans, and what he had done in their sessions. He decided that he had worked honestly and patiently, even if he had lost his client. He felt rueful about that.

Session five

A message was left at the surgery saying that Mrs Evans would be at her appointment, and once again she was there waiting when Derek showed out the client before her. She had more colour, but seemed very nervous, trembling slightly, and greatly embarrassed at 'letting down' – in her words – the therapist. With repeated apologies, she explained that a rich client had taken her and her husband to Italy in his private plane, and was negotiating to buy her business and give her a consultancy role, plus use of one of the villas for the winter months. All this had happened at great speed, her mobile did not work from abroad, she did not have the surgery telephone number, and so on.

Derek: I feel rather amazed and certainly happy that you are telling me an almost fairy tale ending to your story. Like the fairy godmother, this client of yours seems to have recognised you for what you really are. [*She began to cry and struggled to stop.*] It seems very natural to me that you should feel emotional about such a big change coming.

Mrs Evans: It's what you said about seeing what I really am. I don't want to cry, I might break down. I can't stop.

Derek: I hope I'm recognising you for what you really are when I say that I think you are very good at stopping crying. Seeing you now, I guess that you are not as good at letting yourself go on. [*She cried for almost five minutes, sobbing deeply for much of the time. He watched her quietly and finally commented*] I notice how you are going quieter. It sounds as if you have nearly had your cry for the moment. What difference do you notice in yourself now?

He paid attention to her ability to let her organism rather than an intellectual top-dog control her, as seemed so clearly demonstrated here. But she stayed agitated, and by the middle of the session had confessed that she and her husband had not been whisked off to Italy at all. The confession cost her enormous shame. Derek searched himself for what he might have done to provoke her into such an elaborate and seemingly out-of-character lie.

Gradually she told how she felt overwhelmingly grateful to him for the first two sessions, because, in her words, he was the first person who had really listened to her in her life. Derek was privately amazed, as she had seemed so hostile at times. Then the opening of negotiations with the possible buyer of her business had made her feel that she did not need any more therapy. Derek's letters had then weighed on her conscience, so that she had concocted a cover story to let her come back to see him, when she sensed that she still feared breakdown, even with good news promised.

Mrs Evans: I shouldn't have done it.

Derek: I feel touched, that you valued me enough to bother to make up that story. And I admire that you told me that you had. [*He smiled.*] We're looking each other in the eye now. Two people who meet for a very short time, and who recognise each other.

Mrs Evans: I'm not out of the wood yet. I'm not sleeping much, and I still get that giddiness if I forget to do the breathing exercise you taught me. But I get a lot of benefit from it.

Derek: Well, that tells you something about dealing with the giddiness, anyway. And now my mind goes back to the story about being whisked away to Italy. I experienced it almost as a present: a way of saying that only something very extreme would keep you from what you think of as letting me down. For a moment you looked like a young child as you told me.

Mrs Evans: I'm not going to talk about it here, it's past and I don't need to go over it. But when I was eight, I felt I let my mother down. She was the breadwinner and had lost her job and she must have been very lonely. I told her I was a star in the school play and I hid after school every day and pretended I had been at rehearsals. But of course there wasn't a play and so I got into a lot of trouble. I've never told anyone that before. There's no need for it to go any further.

Derek: It won't. [*Derek needed to portmanteau all this information into something potentially useful to Mrs Evans, in the context of BGT.*] A difference I see between me and your mother is that I haven't lost my job. I am not lonely or needy in that way. But both of us are people who feel concern and warmth for you, though in very different ways. And a message I make of your Italian aeroplane story is that you feel concern for me, at a time when you are very lonely and beleaguered yourself. You've shown me that you could feel for her in that scene from when you were eight. I think about your needs too. If you could face her now, what would you want to say to her?

Mrs Evans: I said I wasn't going to talk about it here.

Derek: [*smiles*] And then you did. In a way, I'm not asking you to talk about it. I'm suggesting a way of taking something forward, something that is stuck.

She turned to an empty chair and in guarded language, but with great emotion, said that she felt her mother had had to stop trusting that she could be the adult, the provider, and so Mrs Evans had had to stop being a child. The dialogue moved on to her love for her mother and her father, and ended with her managing to thank both for recognition they had given her in other ways, and happy moments from earlier childhood. In the last few minutes of the session, she told Derek that she believed her whole way of being was dictated by this episode.

Derek: And what do you sense you are doing with that episode now?

Mrs Evans: It seems like a piece of ice that's out of the fridge and is melting away in the sunlight. I can't tell you.

Derek: You are telling me now. And I am hearing you. And because I am not as needy as you describe your mother, it's enough gratification for me to see you – melting in the sunshine. There *is* an exchange between us, one with a lot of pleasure in it for me. In a way, there really is a play and you really are the star in it here.

Derek sensed that the episode she had told and partly re-enacted towards him was so pivotal in her dealing with her fear of breakdown, that he must comment on the present. He responded from what could be described as 'the place of real relationship' (Buber, 1970; Clarkson, 1989; Rogers, 1961).

If she could be aware of Derek's uninvasive and appropriate responses, and aware that these belonged in the sunshine, in warmth, rather than in the fridge she described, he hoped she might be able to add his esteem of her to her own self-esteem. He did not want to increase her feelings of shame, so all this he kept in the realm she had allowed him into – one where reticence was respected, and some allusions not explored.

Follow-up

Mrs Evans was keen to return very soon for her follow-up session. Derek bargained her into waiting two months. He supposed that she would need at least that assimilation time for dealing in particular with what had emerged in the fifth session. He also hoped that any transferential feelings for him, rather likely with such a defended person who had allowed herself to be so confiding to him, would fade to some extent in eight or nine weeks.

In some ways, she seemed sober when the follow-up arrived. The MS had been more in evidence after her husband had caught an infection, and her house was being fitted with the handholds and other equipment that proclaim disability. But her business was being passed on in a way that gave her an occasional role as consultant. Breakdown was no longer an issue. Good feelings to Derek were there, it seemed, partly shown in a large house plant she brought as a present, giving it with slightly tearful thanks.

Mrs Evans: You don't know what you've done for me. I can't explain it to you.

Derek: You did something important for yourself, I saw. Now I'm reminded of when someone has just had a baby, and wants to hug the doctor. He's very very pleased, as I am for you …

Mrs Evans: But he's got more ladies waiting in the delivery room.

Derek: And you have something new, a new understanding and strength, that will stay with you all your life. Thank you very much for the plant.

Derek felt that this analogy had been well understood by Mrs Evans, since she supplied the additional reference to the other clients waiting for him. On her range scales she marked herself as in better state than she had predicted by this stage. Her husband and a neighbour, whom she had appointed as observers, averaged her ratings between them. Derek reported that finally he felt pleased with himself when he reflected on the whole episode.

Conclusion

When asked in supervision, Derek admitted that he supposed the overall good outcome from this fragmented piece of work was probably mostly to do with his own empathy, in the face of a good deal of rejection. His supervisor agreed, adding that his competence must not be forgotten either.

Some of the frustrations and limitations of brief therapy are shown here, as well as the amount that can be achieved with some people in a short time.

Practice points

There are lessons to be learnt from this case study, which was chosen from very many that look more straightforward.

Derek's own emotionality, examined in supervision and in the sessions where Mrs Evans failed to appear, is an example of how much can sometimes be learned from what is projected onto the therapist. Whether this is described in terms of projective identification, parallel process or countertransference is perhaps not very important. The heart of the matter is that there is often a co-creation of feelings when two people talk intimately. **Emotions may on occasion say more about the system or the other person than about the person experiencing them.**

This case study also shows the value of **persisting in an empathic dialogic stance**, in the face of non-co-operation or hostility.

It illustrates that **the relationship between the client and therapist still exists, even through missed appointments or even abandonment of the work**. It can be hard for BGT therapists to stay in contact with this truth, when they work hard and then do not see someone again, or know why, or receive any thanks.

Another feature illustrated here is **the high value there may be in one short scene in the therapy**. Mrs Evans is a reminder of Tallon's belief that many people who do not return to therapy do so because they feel they have been helped enough. To Derek, it was frustrating that what seemed a very large and life-changing confession and insight happened here in the fifth session. It is arguable that a long working-through would have been of benefit to Mrs Evans, as well as giving her support through a difficult time, and allowing for her to plan for what next to do positively in her life.

8

The Brief Gestalt Therapy Group

There are many similarities between BGT in individual and in group settings. The differences are large enough, as well, to merit separate consideration. This chapter will be partly theoretical and to a larger extent methodological, and will be fleshed out by the group case study that follows.

As indicated in Chapter 1, group therapy appears in many cases to be of both immediate and lasting value to participants. The study by Vevers and Hemming (1995) indicates persistence of therapeutic gain, and marked reduction in visits to the doctor's surgery, after attendance at a 10-week Gestalt therapy group. Evans (1999) reports a 25 per cent re-referral rate among mentally-ill patients after his first brief Gestalt group – this in a population where the so-called revolving door policy, of speedy discharge from mental hospital in the expectation of possibly frequent re-referral, would anticipate a far higher rate.

An increase in the amount of group therapy available can be argued therefore to be an appropriate response to the increasing demand for psychological attention to the difficulties of many patients in Primary Care. Not only might this be appropriate, but cost-effective too. Ten weekly two-hour groups for 12 people involve 20 hours of professional time, or 40 if two leaders are used. Six sessions of individual time for each of these same people would require 72 hours of a professional's time.

What may be of equal or more interest to doctors or employers is the amount of lasting change for the better that can be experienced by and witnessed in participants. This statement deserves expansion.

Some advantages of group over one-to-one therapy

Most psychological difficulties are evidence of problems, in Gestalt language, of autonomy and contact. Autonomy, in ordinary English, is the sense of being responsible for oneself, of responding to one's own values and needs. Contact here means the ways in which people deal with each other and the world.

Most people vary their way of interacting from one person to another. Behaviour may be in one style towards the perhaps slightly authoritarian or parental projections a client has to the therapist. To people perceived as strangers, as peers, or as junior, she may be quite other, successful with some, and dysfunctional with others.

In one-to-one work, the client gains awareness and perhaps finds new ways to get on with the therapist. But however skilled the therapist, he cannot authentically be all things. He cannot be more than himself with the client. This problem is largely resolved when the client is working as part of a group, in which there is a range of other people, all with their possibly rigid and inevitably diverse expectations of what responses to give and receive.

Each member of the group is likely to construe others in the range of categories she has invented to handle the environment as she sees it. One member may have the out-of-awareness assumption that if she smiles nicely, other people will do what she wants them to. Another perhaps assumes that unless she throws her weight about, she will not even be noticed. Another has hit on self-effacement, to the point of invisibility, as his way of keeping out of trouble. The culture clash of all these expectations meeting, and probably being frustrated, is potentially a rich seam of discovery and change for each of the people present in the group.

Another quite different advantage of the group over one-to-one therapy is the recognition of **commonality**. It is a touching revelation to many people to discover that they are not unique in what they see as their inadequacies. Nor are they the only ones in the world to harbour grudges, turn sulky, behave badly in their families, or do or feel in the thousand ways of which people are frequently deeply ashamed, and about which they do not easily disclose. What they have seen as uniquely dreadful circumstances in parts of their lives sometimes appear in a different perspective as other people's lives are revealed.

This commonality at best will develop into a feeling of **belonging**. Some writers differentiate this feeling from other forms of love. What is meant here is to do with knowing, valuing and recognising other group members, and being known and valued and recognised by them. Warmth and affection are not necessarily part of this sense. It is the family feeling that members count, both when they are seeming trustworthy and rewarding, and also when they are not for a time a pleasure to be with.

What is here termed belonging, Schutz (1966) calls **inclusion**, a word used with wearyingly different meanings in different psychologies. It is used here to mean the sense of affiliation that has less expression in many modern lives than when people lived for the most part in smaller and less mobile communities. It can be an antidote to self-centredness and selfishness, as the reality of several other people besides themselves takes on value for group members. A doctor who led 10-week groups for some of his patients comments:

> So, is this type of therapy relevant in primary care? The patients in the group presented with a wide range of psychosocial issues commonly seen in general practice such as relationship problems, social phobias, benzodiazepine dependence, unresolved grief, stress, psychosomatic disorders and depression.

> Treating them in one group has an advantage over the reductive labeling medical diagnosis. If the group member sees others sharing their problems, he or she may be able to find similar problems in themselves, producing a much more realistic picture of what they may have to do. Further, they may also notice how they are able to listen and help others and by doing this they can see their particular problem in a greater perspective, a factor described ... as 'universality'. This is not so readily achieved in individual counseling. (Vevers and Hemming, 1995: 2)

Another advantage of group work is **beneficent comparison**. Other people's troubles or maladies may seem to give perspective to what is troubling other members of a group. Compassion may well be evoked when the tribulations of others are told. Distress is often a thorough antidote to rivalry, and provokes co-operative feelings in a way that is not available in one-to-one work.

Vicarious learning is a rich aspect of group therapy. An experiment undertaken by one person provides vivid material for reflection to all the others. It may as well act as an encouragement to other people to experiment. In this way **beneficent competition** is a likely component of any group session.

In a group, **stimulus** in general is more novel, varied and less subtly controllable than in the pair. The excitement and growth that is a desideratum of Gestalt Therapy is the more provoked by hearing a range of perceptions and experiencing a range of responses.

Underlying group theory in BGT

The groups in which Perls demonstrated some of his experimental Gestalt Therapy techniques (1969, 1973) are not a model for current Gestalt group practice. He worked for the most part with one participant at a time, using the other people present as audience and occasionally as commentators. His intention was to demonstrate individual therapy to a group of people.

Current BGT group leader styles differ markedly from one practitioner to another, and at best do not reduce the scope of the group in the way Perls arguably did. What is attempted here is an outline of a framework of theory that may help bring about good therapeutic outcomes, and coherent ways of organising the field, in the minds of the people in them.

Theories of group behaviour have been proposed by people from many different disciplines, who place emphasis on different aspects of group life. A social scientist perspective comes from Bradford et al.'s (1964) humanistic view of group development, influenced by Kurt Lewin. A psychologist, Schutz (1966) suggests the forms of behaviour necessary for group and individual to flourish. Both these are examples of some of the theory sources congenial to BGT.

To be of use, theory needs to encompass three aspects of behaviour and perception available in the group:

1. The **intrapersonal** level, as in individual therapy. In other words, this means the unique experience of any one group member.

    Keith arrives at the group and confesses with shame that he is so paralysed with fear at the thought of addressing a learned society that he has pleaded another engagement, and probably lost the chance of a wanted academic post. In dialogue with the leader, he becomes aware of his complicated feelings towards another candidate for the post. He catharts some of this feeling, understands the connection to rivalry with his brother, and resolves to say that he can after all take on the important speaking engagement.

2. The **interpersonal** level, as members interact, and discover how they react to each other, openly or guardedly, warmly or coldly, and so forth. Power and intimacy are two potentially informative dimensions of interpersonal discovery in a BGT group.

    Working at interpersonal level, Keith might hear from other group members how they perceived him, so his sense of himself becomes more informed. Then an experiment might be undertaken. Keith might choose the members to whom he feels he can speak confidently and do so. Or he might do the opposite, find those with whom he is less at ease, and explore with them how he creates what he calls his paralysis.

3. **Group** level is a rich aspect of therapeutic discovery, clearly only available in a group. Drawing on psychoanalytic theory, the group itself can be construed as organism rather than field (Bion, 1961). Bion is referred to by many writers on Gestalt in groups. He could hardly be a more id-focused theorist, in contrast to the ego focus of Gestalt. However, the differences between apparently almost opposite understandings are sometimes less fundamental than they first appear.

Versions of family systems theories make another organisation of the field (Kempler, 1973; Satir, 1972; Zinker, 1977), again looking at the group's influence on the individual as well as the converse. Attention is given in such theories to the influence on behaviour and perception of history, position, preconception and often fear-based organisation. The group as a force field, possibly in relation to other force fields, is thus brought to awareness.

Working at group level with the same issue, Keith might let himself imagine what the present therapy group evokes in his fantasy. Other people shut their eyes and add their images. One is of a dragon lashing its tail and snapping its jaws, ready to destroy anything outside itself. Keith connects this image to part of his schooldays, and to the audience he dreads. Unacknowledged competitiveness, and fear of failure comes into the open and is understood as the polarity of the friendly working alliance and trust more often commented on before. This shared fear helps Keith feel less overcome by his fear of the other group.

Insight into Bion's theory of small groups is taught at the Tavistock Institute in London, and other analytically-oriented institutes by way of tightly-bounded groups in which a consultant only ever intervenes at group process level. But one particular therapeutic or teaching method does not always have to be intrinsic to the theory it was designed to illustrate.

Many of the speculations offered as interpretations by the consultant in such a group can be made by BGT group members who have been taught to look out for and respect the images that dart into their minds, and the feelings that may suffuse them in ways that seem unaccountable. In other words, the power-sharing theory and methods of Gestalt are not incompatible with the powerful speculations of Bion's theory.

This point is made in part to encourage readers to see how they can use what is of value in other disciplines, not necessarily by swallowing whole the language and the methods of those disciplines. The river banks that make the boundaries of Gestalt are not immutable, but should not be attacked with bulldozers. Rather they will at best accommodate themselves over time by an accretion here, an erosion there.

This ability to move fluently between wide and narrow gestalt formation tends to maximise the learning available in this setting. The assimilation and adaptation of psychoanalytic theory here is an enrichment of both the dialogic and the Perlsian theories-in-action.

Another pervasive but until the last few years less-acknowledged influence in BGT is Moreno's (1953) brilliantly inventive 'sociotherapy'. This theory and practice of intervention into groups and systems, rather than at individual level, is arguably more urgently needed in the world even than when it was invented. It makes inspirational reading for BGT practitioners in groups.

Teaching in BGT groups

In the early meetings of a BGT group, the teaching of Gestalt concepts can be useful in several ways. It establishes a common language and frame of reference, and thus establishes something approaching parity between therapist and members. Perhaps almost as importantly, it makes the group into an obviously educational experience, where in the UK culture at least, therapy is popularly often seen to be only for the mad and the bad.

Ken Evans (1999) reports a successful 20-week group intervention with patients with mental illness, where he began by teaching Perlsian Gestalt concepts, centring on these statements about self-responsibility:

1. This is how I am;
2. I choose to be this way;
3. If I want I can behave differently.

There is scope in a BGT group for spending some time in overt teaching, and even for naming the group a 'training and therapy group'. However, structure can be a defence against therapist anxiety. The urge to teach always needs to be evaluated in the light of the needs of the group, rather than those of the therapist. Teaching is easy. It is probably well within the therapist's competent area of knowledge, and outside that of the clients. Therapy is by contrast likely to be far less predictable, and by no means guaranteed to stay in a comfortable area of competence for the practitioner.

Getting into the group

Many British people shrink from the idea of group therapy. Images from the film *One Flew Over The Cuckoo's Nest* are likely to be cited. Paranoia may be provoked in the otherwise balanced and trusting. So it seems worth giving much attention to the introduction to potential members of the whole idea of attending a brief group.

One comparatively pain-free way adopted by some practitioners is to run groups alongside individual therapy. Clients are commonly first seen in individual sessions, then invited, if that seems appropriate, to join a 10-week group. The 10-week groups run three times a year, in academic term times. Clients are free to re-apply for a second or third term if they wish. Their application has to be allowed by the therapist. This deals with the 'joiners', those people who try to join Weightwatchers though they are as thin as beanpoles, or cycling clubs though they cannot stay upright on a bicycle. In some settings, for example, with people recovering from alcohol dependency, there is much to be said for encouraging members to linger in the group. For many others, it is less likely that the group will become a beneficent addiction. Two terms or even three may nevertheless still be of great value for those who are less speedy than others at achieving the changes they are involved in.

If clients are likely to be recommended – by a doctor, manager or lecturer – to try a group, the name of the group may of itself have a pleasant or unpleasant impact. Some practitioners therefore settle for using such camouflage names as the Tuesday Group, or Sally's Group or the Denman Hall Group. Behind such anonymity there needs to be some explanation, possibly in leaflets, preferably by people.

At best, the person who will mainly be in charge of the group is known and trusted in the institution where it will happen. It should be part of the work of student and workplace counsellors to make themselves known and approachable. Then it is more likely that people will cheer up at the possibility of attending a group they lead.

In this context, it may be said that fifth-year students of Gestalt Psychotherapy are very suitable for placements as apprentice or assistant therapists. The work will be of benefit to them as well as the group members and other professionals. This argument must be of interest to fund-holders (Wessler and Wessler, 1997).

For therapists in Primary Health Care, it is harder to be known to the large numbers of patients in a practice. So it is in this setting that the two-tier, individual and group design, is of special use. Against the extra cost can be set the reality that many of the people who are referred within a GP practice for counselling are distressed enough to be using a good deal of doctors' time in somatisation of psychological states. Their constant re-appearance in the waiting room is evidence that the doctors' best ministrations do not, indeed perhaps cannot, deal adequately with whatever is troubling them.

Making a start

For our purposes, the group is assumed to last about 10 weeks, with each session lasting two hours. If the resources are available, perhaps in the form of a reliable volunteer or student assistant, an all-day Saturday or Sunday meeting may usefully be designed in at the outset. This meeting may at times be held in a different setting away from the institution. It will give scope for more variety of experiment.

The writer recalls one such group in a Primary Healthcare Trust who could not find the alternative setting they had decided to search for, for their all-day meeting. Instead they organised themselves into a walk in the country, based on a Thames-side pub where two physically-disabled members could wait while the others explored the river and then returned for a pub lunch. The whole arrangement and negotiation of this was by the members of a group the members acknowledged to be characterised by timorousness and loneliness. Behaviour and perception was, they decided, to be noted and experimented with, and talked through at the next weekly two-hour meeting.

Designing a group culture

In the first or early meetings, norms or ground rules can usefully be invented and possibly made into a written charter. The first agreement that needs to be reached, in the interests of promoting trust, is on **confidentiality**.

The emphasis on self-responsibility that is a strength of Gestalt, means that the leader is advised to elicit from the group what confidentiality contract is to be made. The result may be exactly what she would have proposed if asked. It may have taken 30 minutes rather than one to agree it. But if she suggested the wording, that would be an imposition. If it comes from the group, it is owned by them, and power-sharing has begun to be a value in reality in the group.

What follows is a list of some of the ground rules that have proved helpful in concentrating the minds of members of many Brief Gestalt groups. They are meant as a checklist rather than an inviolable codex.

Various norms can be set about speech itself, from very strict limitations on verb forms or reifying or much else, to 'anything goes'. My preference is for careful attention to speech forms, as these are thought forms and action forms too.

The use of I and you, rather than impersonal constructions and the third person, are to be recommended.

Openness can be an enormous facilitator of ease, enjoyment and learning in a group. However, a requirement of openness is very rarely appropriate. It can be tantamount to requiring non-swimmers to swim the first time they enter the water. One or two might succeed. Many more are likely to form an aversion to or terror of the swimming pool. **An awareness of ease or difficulty in self-disclosure is arguably of importance**, and can be recommended as a private self-evaluation, if people are very wary, particularly in the early stages of a group.

Some groups decide to require or invite members to **report the feeling that accompanies any statement**. They may go further and invite people to say 'I am blocking my feeling in saying X', rather than say the more common, 'I don't feel anything when I say X'. In this perhaps mechanistic way, members can remind themselves of when and perhaps how they keep part of their experience out of awareness. Or they may notice more vividly the feeling that inevitably accompanies thought and action.

English has been described as a language that is very rich as a descriptor of external experience, and poorer as an accurate conveyor of perception. But this accurate description of perception is often central to therapeutic gain, and so worth striving for.

Both to point this up, and overcome confusion, John Weir (Houston, 1998a) invented what he first called 'responsibility language', and later 'percept language'. This is a cumbersome new grammar and phrasing to be used in I–Thou communication. That is to say, it makes it easy to distinguish between observation and projection or assumption, by requiring the speaker to pay very close attention to her phenomenology. In this way every statement becomes specific, and even everyday speech acts are unpacked, as in these examples.

Instead of saying 'Thanks for the birthday card', a 'percept' answer might be rendered, 'I am making myself tearful, noticing that you remembered me. I have you as the tender-hearted part of me, that wants to give pleasure'.

Percept language demands that responsibility is taken for the self: 'I make myself cry', rather than, 'You made me cry'. Projections are owned as they occur. The last sentence in the quotation above says 'I have you as', rather than 'You are'. Again, rather than acknowledge where the projection lands, it is owned: 'the tender-hearted part of me, that wants to give pleasure'. It can be seen that every statement in percept language will be immediate, original and personal.

'Goodbye', likewise, will never be the same statement twice in percept language, as it is an expression of the phenomenology of a particular farewell. On one occasion it might be, 'I am making myself happy, imagining you enjoying the sun and the mountains on your holiday'. At another time or to another person it might be, 'I am making my stomach cold, knowing we shall not meet again soon. I am frightening myself with fantasies that one of us will die'.

Week-long groups have been run with this form of speech prescribed as the only one. This may be a taxing ambition. An invitation to stay in the mode for half an hour may be enough to alert most members of a group to nuances of meaning in their own dialogue, that in ordinary English stay obscure.

Accuracy of speech is an aid to vividness of perception. Experiments that distinguish between sensing, thinking and feeling often help people use words more accurately. **Feel**, for example, is often used confusingly to mean think, consider, guess, assume, accuse.

Another fruitful area of speech awareness is to do with dropped syllables, cant phrases and the thousand often irritating fandangles people use to hide feelings or ward off the other. 'You know', 'like', well, 'sort of', 'er', 'at the end of the day', 'anyway', 'kindalike', 'I dunno'. What to look for here is not some literary standard of correctness, but heightened awareness of linguistic evasions of the present.

In Middle English there was supposed to be a special devil whose torment was to go about with a great sack, picking up all these dropped syllables. In the editing channels of BBC radio, editors used to be condemned to go through tapes and snip 'ers' from the pronouncements of public figures, or even actors, before their words were transmitted. A cutting room floor covered in celluloid 'ers' and 'actuallies' was a salutary sight.

Other experiments may enhance people's ability to distinguish between what they observe and what they suppose (Houston, 1998a). 'You are wrinkling your nose', for example, is an observable event. 'You don't approve of what I am saying', may be the deduction from that evidence, that is offered up as if it was a clever observation of fact, rather than a projection on the part of the speaker.

Other ground rules may be to do with **receptivity**. Alongside the above encouragement to speak accurately and own projections rather than pass judgements freely and in a way confusing to all parties, there can be an attempt at **hearing out** whatever is said, rather than interrupting and defending or contradicting. William Blake's notion that **everything that can be imagined is an aspect of the truth** is salutary. An unwelcome statement may turn out to have relevance for the object of it. It will certainly have relevance for the speaker. Early in the life of any group there is a good deal of repetitive spadework to be done, as cheerfully and lightly as appropriate, to remind people to leave ordinary social modes of conversation, and experiment instead with those outlined in the norms they have agreed.

In some groups such attention to forms of speech may seem burdensome. If it does, then it is not to be recommended. However, attention to language is attention to a major channel of communication, and a major potential source of confusion. Where it has been out of fashion in Gestalt, a lack of effectiveness does seem to have followed.

Continuing culture

The groundwork, then, has been to agree with people what they are here for, and how they are to go about their task. If this groundwork is well done, members of the group are more likely to take charge of their own learning and experimentation as the weeks go by. The therapist may share the dismay of others at the ending of a 10-week course. Her dismay will have the extra dimension of supposing she may have to start the teaching part of the work, partly outlined above, when she starts the following 10-week group. If the contract allows for some members to stay on for another term, then her work will be reduced greatly. A climate will be set faster by several people, some of them group members, than by one leader.

What has been described so far is likely to make for a secure group, who have had spelt out to them the connection between 'response-ability', 'contact', and coming to the various changes each of them has designed, as the next paragraphs describe.

Generating evidence

As described in Chapter 4, a focus on just one or two areas of interest for each person helps everyone to stay engaged. Again, these foci may be arrived at tentatively in the first session. In the group people can talk in pairs or threes, before writing down their foreground therapeutic interests. Their present position in relation to each difficulty can be plotted on a 10-point scale, from 0 to 9. Zero will signify no difficulty; 9 means severe difficulty. In a different colour, and after consultation in the pair or sub-group, a long-term goal place on the scale can be marked, as well as other marks for where the person wants to be by the end of the 10-week course, and in a year or six months.

Another advantage of the group shows here. Members can if they wish undertake to monitor or prompt each other in their tasks, both in sessions, and in the intervals between sessions.

Each week or fortnight, a short time can be assigned in the group session to this sub-group work. In turn, people show their chart, and mark where they have moved, whether toward or away from where they want to be. Also, the partner or other two mark, on their copies of this chart, where they judge the protagonist to have arrived. This mark may or may not tally with the protagonist's. In the light of what is marked, the pair or three may modify their ways of helping and monitoring each other.

To avoid lost papers, it may be advisable to have the group assign one person to be the secretary or keeper of the papers. If he can find a place within the building where they meet, to lodge these documents, risk of losing them is reduced, and confidentiality is more obviously kept.

In this way, group members have access to their own and other people's impressions of what they are doing. This record is not made outside group time, but is a valid research project intrinsic to the work of the group.

Tasks for the therapist in Brief Gestalt Therapy groups

A good number of these tasks have been implied or specifically described already. Many of them would not be necessary, or perhaps even desirable, in one-to-one work. Quantity changes quality.

Group therapy needs in some respects to be qualitatively different from individual work. Otherwise, serial individual therapy may become the mode. The protagonist of any moment may feel gratified, while all the other group members wait in an invisible but jealous queue for their share of the therapist's attention. The therapist may begin to perceive herself as the old woman who lived in a shoe, who had so many children she did not know what to do. And we know the hostile response to such demands that lady arrived at.

Evans (1999) describes a phase of his 20-session group devoted to such one-to-one work. A rule of thumb is to give some individual trainer time to each member at some point in the group's life, if the members are all first-timers to therapy. If they have some experience, their development may be served better by encouraging them to work with each other rather than the leader or leaders.

Gestalt work in a group certainly involves attention to the individual. But this occurs at best alongside attention to the larger gestalts of sub-group and whole-group interaction. At least as much time as in one-to-one therapy needs to be spent in process comment. At first this may come from the therapist. At best, the task is shared with the rest of the group as other people's awareness is raised in this field.

The therapist's task is to stay here and now, and to frustrate every attempt by group members to avoid that revelatory area.

Contact and the group

'Contact' is the word used to describe a central focus of attention in this therapy. It is meant to include all aspects of people's style of interaction. Much of the time that involves speech, eye contact and some gesturing and body stance. Its root meaning, obviously, is touch itself. The Gestalt assumption is that a vast amount of social talk is a verbal substitute for caressing, cuffing, pinching, punching, stroking, kissing, and a thousand other forms of touch commonly outlawed in what we call civilised conversation.

The presence of a number of people in a therapeutic setting tends towards feelings of safety around touch. Members are less likely to interpret it as sexual than they might in a closed room with only one other person. Even if they do admit to sexual suspicions or unease, the subject is likely to be easier to talk through among many, than with just one other perhaps defending herself or himself.

One of the many therapeutic advantages of Gestalt Therapy in a group is that physical experiments are likely to be acceptable. In one-to-one work, high anxiety may be an unlooked-for result of the therapist's touching the client. Though some Gestalt therapists nevertheless use touch in this setting, others (including the writer) generally refrain.

In a group, physical contact can enable the pre- or non-verbal meanings of much speech to be experimented with freely. For example, an edgy group member resorts to psycho-babble and says that she does not experience this as 'a very holding environment'. 'Who would you like to hold you here?' is an economical Gestalt response that invites a present, concrete experiment to replace the generalised resentment the member has chosen to cloak her feelings of exclusion.

In a similar way, a quiet member of a group suddenly launches into a long statement of how she can understand perfectly well what is going on for some other member who is under attack at that moment. Rather than go on listening to a dialogue in which the pair refine the nuances of what is being understood, the group leader may suggest that the first speaker finds a physical way to convey what she is saying. Discovering that a hand on the other person's shoulder, or a hug, gives a complete and indeed self-gratifying expression of all these inadequate words, may be part of a strong and lasting perceptual change. Love may have re-entered members' awareness. 'We must serve [love] … and make a place for it to dwell'. (Latner, 1995: 49)

Language, we have acknowledged here, is a means of expression of great subtlety. As Stern (1985) among others points out, it has the weakness that it is an efficient conveyor of lies as well as of truth. Except for trained actors, perhaps, it is harder to lie with the body than with words. In another simple and telling experiment possible in a group, two members who have been in conflict and then say they are reconciled, may be seen to glower at each other, or avoid eye contact. They may honestly believe that they no longer bear a grudge, but their body language says otherwise.

Then, perhaps, they are asked to stand and face each other at opposite sides of the room, and then advance slowly, a step at a time, until they are at a distance they find congenial. Their physical sense of appropriate social distance may well surprise them. The different distance perhaps needed by each person is further enlightening. The rest of the group will be of potential help to the pair in commenting on their attitude, in the concrete rather than the abstract meaning of the word.

Another aspect of the therapist's work is to train somewhat insensitive members, or encourage more psychologically-minded ones, in observation. Rather than perceiving in snapshots of isolated moments, they will profit from becoming aware of patterns and sequences of gestures, speech or episodes of interaction. Stern (1985) again is helpful with his theory of 'vitality affect'. This could almost be rendered as the music and cadence of interaction.

Some early childhood models lead people to repeatedly aborting, abruptly stopping dialogue that to that point seemed full of approach and excitement. Others cannot let go or complete the gestalt of an interaction, but linger in repetition and progressively more lame responses. To bring these or myriad other dysfunctional patterns of interaction to full awareness, it may be of great help to have different pairs of people in the group actually dance or physically enact what they have made of an incident, while the protagonist watches.

All manner of experiments, involving several people or all, become possible in the group. A whole group lift of a member who has been through some painful experience, and consents to lie down and be ministered to, can be a powerful healing experience. In one-to-one work no complete equivalent is possible.

The few examples cited here are of experiments likely to be familiar to many Gestalt-trained therapists. They are intended as an introduction for other readers to the range of experiential work that is possible and often an aid to vivid learning in Brief Gestalt Therapy. Chapter 9 includes some explanation of the therapist's experience and strategy.

Summation

In many instances, BGT is more effectively carried on in a group than one-to-one. Co-operation and beneficent comparison and competition are possible there, as they are not in a pair.

How the group is set up will have profound effects on how it proceeds. The leader or pair of leaders need training in group behaviour as well as Gestalt Therapy.

Practice points

BGT group leaders will do well to raise awareness of:

Belonging

Styles of contact

Individual learning goals and progress towards them

Co-operative learning

The detail of particular events in the group, in what can be termed 'narrow gestalt formation'

The larger field of culture, history, background that leads to 'wide gestalt formation'.

Appendix C

Examples of ready-made group experiments

Major and minor goals

This exercise often gives people a sense of their own worth and enthusiasm. To begin, each person thinks of a 'major goal'. This may be where they want to be in their lives in five or ten years' time. It may be the writing of the obituary they would like to have written about them. Time is needed, perhaps to talk in pairs before writing, or sharing in pairs and in the group after writing.

After this, the idea is presented that every action taken in life can be described as a minor goal. Each one either supports, moves towards, or moves away from the 'major goal'. The rest of the meeting, or of each person's day, can be looked at in this way, and if necessary re-designed in some respects.

Cornstarch experiment

In what seems an unlikely circumstance in the British Isles, but more feasible in America, is the good weather to invite a cornstarch or wallpaper paste exercise. This needs to be done outdoors, with the participants in old and washable clothes. They sit in a circle on the ground, blindfolded or with their eyes shut. In silence, a fair-sized sheet of drawing paper is placed on the ground or on a table in front of each person. They are asked to explore the paper with their hands, imagining it to be their world. Then a dollop of wallpaper paste is put in the middle of the paper. Some people may retroflect, and keep the paste within the paper. Others may begin to play or aggress, and a wide-ranging blind contest may follow. Such an active and evocative exercise may generate enough material for 10 weeks' work, at intrapsychic, interpersonal and group level.

Fantasy experiment

1. Say that a silent fantasy is going to be suggested, and that no one need take part unless interested.
2. Invite people to relax, loosen tight clothing, find an easy position to sit or loll, and shut their eyes. Deliberate tightening and loosening of groups of muscles all through the body probably helps this process, as can the invitation to notice the darkness behind the shut eyelids.
3. After some attention to easy breathing, give another assurance that people can tune out your voice at any time.

4. Make suggestions that are open-ended. For example, say 'Imagine that you are getting smaller and smaller, and lighter and lighter. Notice how that feels. Notice what is happening. Where are you? What weather is there? This is your fantasy, so you can have whatever weather you need to'. You need to make pauses between these statements and questions, to allow images to develop in people's minds. A future-oriented fantasy might continue: 'You are high above the world now. Notice how fast or slowly you are travelling. Notice what you can see beneath you. You can land wherever you like. Take your time and bring yourself down somewhere. Really notice this place, and use your power to change it in any way you want to'.
5. After continuing the fantasy to give a likelihood of interesting discoveries, recommend people to bring themselves back to now, by moving slightly and taking their own time to bring themselves out of their reverie, into their own bodies and this place.
6. Ask them to talk in pairs, if a group, or to you, in individual work, about the fantasy. When they have told some of the story of it, or the process of their difficulty if they did not find images easily, begin to apply their discoveries to now and the future. Questions like, 'What is this like in your life now? What in this fantasy would you like to enjoy in your life now? How could you begin to do that? How might you stop yourself? What did you learn about your usual state of tension from doing this exercise?' Perls et al. (1951) spoke of **directions** that are indicated by daydreams. Being a millionaire, in his time, might be an impossibility. But someone with that dream knows at least that he is invested in making money. He can set to and do that, or sit and mope because he has not achieved the ultimate point of being as rich as Croesus.

9

A BGT Group Case Study

This report of part of the life of a 10-week Gestalt Therapy group is meant to illustrate some of the ways the Gestalt therapist may work in such a gathering. It is a camouflaged account, and one that often highlights difficulties, rather than illustrating the preponderant ease of communication and goodheartedness generally experienced in such gatherings of distressed people who are being taken seriously and warmly. Laura Perls recommended a sensitivity of approach that amounted almost to the invention of a particular therapy for a particular person. So in a group, there needs to be a tuning of approach to each member, and to the unique whole, the group created by these members and this therapist.

This account, therefore, is not meant as a formula for such a group. At best, it brings to awareness some likely stages and events, some possible but less likely ones, and some ways in which one BGT therapist has responded to those stages and events.

To look at some specifics: the introduction of ground rules like those spoken of in the last chapter is optional, even being seen by some as authoritarian (Parlett and Hemming, 1996). Devices such as the 'check-in' or 'go-round' at the beginning of meetings, quoted here, are programmatic. In many groups I have not used them. Instead I have attempted to do as I was required in training: to hold the whole group in awareness. This requires an instant registering of who is being silent, who is acting differently this week, who excites a response from the trainer. The advantage of this free system is that the group begins with a creative void. The character of the group will emerge as speakers licence themselves to speech or silence. Tendencies to lead or be led will soon show, and the power dynamics of the group will be in evidence for comment and possible change.

The go-round is likely to remove anxiety, and certainly offers, for some members, some comfortable upholstering of the creative void. A plus is that it also makes very clear, early on, what is going on for each member. Each person expresses herself, or makes explicit that she refuses to. Each person in a sense steps over a threshold into speech, and may thus be more at ease to speak again. A disadvantage is that it may allow a serial reporting of out-of-context experience, unless the therapist is ready to help people connect all they tell to the group, to the present, and their own work topic.

In the third session of the group described here, the go-round is omitted, and a retroflective member is overlooked in the rest of the session. Readers will work out for themselves what value they put on this event, or on either of the styles discussed here.

Kate is an experienced BGT worker, who will focus for much of the time on the way in which people's behaviour in this group throws light on other parts of their lives, and on the difficulties that have brought them here. She sees each person's style of getting on with others to be fascinating and worthy of respect, however dysfunctional it may seem to other members.

By encouraging everyone in the group to listen openly to all they can pick up from each other, she hopes to move the group towards the dialogic, learning mode that she deems likely to bring about great insight, and perhaps some of the safety and affection most people need. Underpinning her dialogic method are two somewhat opposed theories of group behaviour. She finds Wilfred Bion's (1961) notions of the unaware group process of use at some moments when she wants to make sense of puzzling events. And she finds Schutz's (1966) ideas of three needed forms of behaviour in the group (Houston, 1998b) a useful way of describing what may be lacking or too much in evidence. Belonging, being or feeling in or out, suspicious or fraternal, is the first of Schutz's areas of focus. Then comes everything to do with power and control. The last on his list is pair formation, a topic on which his view is diametrically opposed to Bion. Arguably both theorists are right and of use to the BGT group practitioner.

Background

The setting is an upstairs room in a Primary Healthcare Trust. All the members have been referred by doctors in the practice. Each of the nine members' stories merits its own case study, but that would involve another book. An attempt is therefore made to be as economical as possible in describing the members, in order to make as much room as possible to show the reader the therapist's responses and perceptions. The aim is not to describe pathology, but to extend the reader's repertoire of therapeutic responses.

The members

When recommended to the group, each member has been offered a short conversation with Kate, the therapist. They have also been given a descriptive leaflet and have filled in a questionnaire. The list here has a thumbnail description, partly quoted from the pre-group questionnaire (unless otherwise specified, members are white and of UK origin):

Dan, 38, Afro-Caribbean, a salesman. Refuses medication, but is hyperactive, controlling and disputatious when he drinks.

Pat, 59, is a civil servant who retired early after bad heart trouble. Goes to many residential courses on alternative therapies and spiritual paths.

Jane, 43, Irish Protestant, a social worker. Wants to be a female leader. Is an out-of-control eater.

Tom, 23, a computer programmer, has an IQ of 150. Can't sustain relationships. Is frightened of sex.

Babs, 27, a teacher. Is quiet, does not keep order well. Stress of father's illness brought her to group.

Ollie, 34, Malaysian, gay. Is overcompliant, anxious. Has high principles.

Clare, 46. Tends to support managers and boss. Is depressive.

Val, 40. Is beautiful, had short training in counselling. Suffers from vestibulitis, thrush, cystitis, frigidity.

Flo, 29, a shop assistant. Has persistent catarrh, irritable bowel syndrome.

The beginning of the first meeting

Clare, Ollie, Tom and Flo arrive on time. The other five members straggle into the room very slightly late, and take the remaining seats in the circle Kate has set up. Kate's opening is put here as if it is all said in one go. In reality, it is interspersed with invitations to the rest to comment and question, and with dealing with these first enquiries.

Kate: I notice how anxious I am – and so glad everyone's arrived. Now you all know the way, so we shall start right on time in future. Before you have a chance to talk, maybe I need to give you some more background than is in the paper you all had. You did get it? [*She stops to register assents and nods from everyone before continuing.*] Your doctors talked to me a bit about each of you. But I have put their notes away on file, and hope I shall not want to go and look them up again. That may sound odd. But one of the ideas in Gestalt Therapy is that everyone takes responsibility for his or her own experience. That's a reality, really, not just an idea. You haven't handed yourselves over for treatment by coming here.

Most of you have shown a lot of doggedness in filling in your questionnaires. You were starting work on yourselves already in doing that. In this group I hope that I can give you more ways of listening to and being with yourselves and each other. I want to do that, rather than pretend to be the mysterious guru who knows it all and dispenses my wondrous wisdom. What we might do first is give everyone a chance to report what's now, what's your present experience. I'd better start.

I'm talking a lot, and maybe I shall go on like that in this first meeting. There's a lot I want you to know, and that you may want me to tell. Then as time goes on, I hope that you learn the ropes enough to sail the ship without having me as captain all the time. As well as that, I notice I'm stopping breathing from time to time. Not exactly a good idea. I'm anxious, and wanting to do well by you, and worrying. That's me now.

The introduction included some appreciation of the other people in the group, their capacities and work. Then, as well as giving some necessary first descriptions of Gestalt assumptions, Kate has, by starting the go-round, shown what she means by reporting present experience. This level of transparency is part of the dialogic method, and contrasts with the group facilitator style in other schools, notably the psychoanalytic.

The weighty word **phenomenological** is used to describe the reporting of internal phenomena or happenings. These include sensations such as sights, sounds and bodily sensations; emotions, such as sadness, happiness or anger, for example. These are Darwinian or categorical emotions, described in Darwin (1872). Vitality affects (Stern, 1985) such as liveliness, lethargy, are noted too, as well as imaginings, memories and other spontaneous mentation. Rational developments of these are not seen as part of phenomenology. So, 'I'm stopping breathing' is a phenomenological report. Kate's comment, 'Not exactly a good idea', is not phenomenological. It is an opinion, implicitly involving abstraction and comparison. Simple direct experience is the subject of phenomenology.

At first hesitantly, people tell their names and volunteer something about themselves. This next quotation illustrates the teaching needed in the early stages of a BGT group:

Flo: [*to Kate*] I thought you'd want to hear about our problems. I have a terrible lot of allergies, and I have irritable bowel syndrome.
Val: Have you? I had, but I think I've cured it.
Clare: I thought that dark patch round your eye was an injury. Is it allergic?
Kate: [*interpolating quickly. To Flo.*] Yes, you've all come to this group hoping to deal with various illnesses and other sorts of distress. And now I ask you to tell about just this moment. It seems strange. But we may be able to find out a lot from doing just that. Let me paraphrase what you said so that the present is more obvious in it. It might be, 'What I'm most in touch with is IBS, and' [this is a guess] 'worries about whether this group will help me'.
Flo: [*to Kate*] Whether *you* can help me, really.

Kate might launch into more theory about self-direction: or the group – not just the therapist – being the instrument of change. Instead, she implicitly offers Flo the help she mentions. From moment to moment, as Kate attempts to stay aware of the whole field of the group and herself, in her somewhat powerful position in it, her need varies between **recognising** and **confronting** different members.

Kate: I guessed at you being worried about me. Was that true?
Flo: Well, I think I was a bit alarmed. And I want to know what this lady …
Val: Val.
Flo: What Val's found to cure IBS. Have you tried Chinese medicine?
Kate: You were alarmed. That was the feeling about me. And perhaps there was another feeling towards Val?

Flo: Not a feeling. I don't like to have feelings very much.
Val: Well, there's your problem in a nutshell. You have IBS instead. I feel so much, so much pain.
Kate: If Flo and Val and I stood up and showed without words what's going on between us …

Kate gets agreement from Flo and Val to experiment, and invites other people to represent the three in interaction. After some hesitation, a physical struggle to be king of the castle is depicted. Flo does not identify with this.

Flo: I really don't want to fight.
Tom: You look as if you've been in one.
Flo: I walked into a door, that's all. I'd so like to make some friends here, and to feel a bit better in myself.
Kate: I remember you put that on your form.

This recognition statement seems needed, Kate decides, rather than more discussion of the process-level control battle evidently well understood by most of the group. The experiment is likely to have taught everyone more about being present, and noticing what is going on besides the words in the group conversation.

Kate has twice interrupted the beginning of a conversation about medical symptoms that was certainly foreground for the speakers. So why stand in the way of this lively present?

The justification is the field. The field here has such elements as the newness of the group; the naivety of most members about Gestalt method; the need for everyone to have a say; Kate's desire to hold people in the present, and frustrate their every attempt to escape. Physically the field is the Health Centre, where physical symptoms are often the currency. In Chapter 1, the attraction of treating doctors' referrals as new visits to a doctor have already been outlined.

As ever in these illustrations, no formula or rule is intended. This example has been chosen, though, to show how some therapists do their best to work in a present-centred style from the very beginning of an episode of therapy. Supervisees not infrequently report frustration with an opening session, adding that they felt it was a bit early to start process comment, insistence on examining the fine structure of perception, or whatever. This procrastination can be called the Deferred Living Principle. 'Letting I dare not wait upon I would' is a dubious practice. It is also one that can continue till the end of the group's life. Beware. I am drawn to yet more comment on this fragment and its implications.

Kate's words could be uttered in many ways and from many stances. She is understood to be interested in everyone in the group, and secure enough that she does not feel rivalrous with them in more than minute homeopathic moments. Thus, what she says is meant as descriptive and invitational. She is co-operative rather than competitive. If she uttered the same words in a way that suggested that she did want to be 'king of the castle', to gain a petty victory (Perls et al., 1951, ch. 9), the group might cave in and lose energy, or be devoted to skirmish rather than the primary tasks of insight and healing.

After everyone has spoken, they set to work in triads, to talk over what focus each person is choosing as a work area for the duration of the group. They set up range scales on these constructs:

Dan: to listen more; to give in rather than take the lead.

Pat: to drink less; to honour his spirituality.

Jane: to control her eating and lose weight; to be less of a bully.

Tom: to be more at ease with women.

Babs: to be more at ease with taking the limelight, instead of hiding behind father's needs.

Ollie: to be able to relax; to be less critical of himself and other people.

Clare: to do what she wants, rather than give in to other people.

Val: to learn from Kate so that she can run similar groups in another practice.

Flo: to find out who she is.

Ollie is made Group Secretary by the other members, and Kate gives him a folder in which the documents can be stored. Choosing a name for the folder, and thereby for the group, is left for next week, by common consent. People also agree, at Dan's suggestion, to look for a phrase or word to describe each session. These are recorded here in the sub-headings.

Some of the rest of the time is spent in brainstorming some ground rules for the group, beginning with confidentiality.

Then people have the chance to divulge to everyone what has been written on the range scales. At the same time, members are invited to set up help or monitoring contracts between themselves. Pat organises an email and telephone list, and volunteers to send it to everyone before next week. Most of the session has gone.

Kate: Has anyone not got anyone else to report to, and talk over your plans?
Babs: I haven't. My father has to be looked after all the time now.
Kate: Do you know what you'd like to do about that?
Babs: It's all right.
Kate: I feel anxious when you say that. [*Babs shrugs*] How do the rest of you react?

Clare: [*to Babs*] It sounds as if you're saying that you don't matter.
Babs: It's not important, really.
Kate: [*to Clare*] So what does that sound like?
Clare: Like, 'I don't matter really'.
Kate: Yes. [*to Babs*] You matter to me. And you need to matter to you. You're the world authority on what's going on for you, after all. And now we've got to the last five minutes of this meeting. Only nine more times together. Let's finish by saying just one or two words each, to describe the feeling you notice most now, after two hours of quite intense work at something totally new to most of you.

Again, principles of BGT group method mean that Kate has kept the whole group in the foreground, rather than being drawn into spending the last minutes of the very first meeting in dialogue with just one member. She has kept the time limit of the group in awareness. She has offered recognition and appreciation of the amount of work people have done.

This group has opted for strict rules about speech forms and present-centred speech generally, and have asked Kate to police this. She has agreed to do so until she is bored, when she will make that clear. The disadvantage of such strictness is that members may hold back from talking, or may take delight in pouncing on each other's deviations. An advantage is, as Robin Skynner (1993) says, 'A tight ship makes a proud crew'; another is that this change of method of conversation often makes for clarity of perception.

Extracts from the second session: Autonomy? Or confluence with Kate's demands?

Everyone else is sitting ready when Kate comes into the room at the time the group is scheduled to begin.

Kate: I notice my spirits lifting, seeing you all look ready to start. If you agree, I suggest we leave those written scales to look at again next week. Now we could make a beginning by hearing who we are today. We've all lived another week of our lives. So what is there for you to say to us?
Val: I'll start, because I usually go last. Kate'd call that an experiment. [*Laughter. She reports phenomenologically. Other people follow suit until all but Ollie have spoken. Kate remarks on this.*]

There is much to be said for leaving it to group members to suggest wanting to work. A statement from the therapist at the beginning, that she will react to people, rather than impose on them, will encourage this style. In this group, that has a majority of members who would in former times have been described as retroflective, Kate is prepared to instigate experiments after consulting. Leaving the members to learn by frustration to ask assertively for what they want, may, in her judgement, take too much of the group's time.

Kate: Ollie, what are you experiencing now?
Ollie: Oh, I was lost in what everyone was saying.
Kate: You were lost. Is that what you want?
Ollie: No. It's like saying I've got no edges. I sort of flow into what's happening.
Pat: But that's very spiritual. I like that. No self.
Ollie: I gave myself HIV, though, by not thinking of myself.
Jane: It's the other person's responsibility. He was criminal.
Pat: I don't see why.
Clare: Let's talk about us, not other people. We can't change them, and we can change us.
Pat: You've persuaded me, dear.

Kate sees the way Clare smiles at Pat, and notes her own dismay that they seem on intimate terms, while she is momentarily angered by Pat's tone and use of the word 'dear'. She puts the thought aside, as her own moralism and prejudice, and lets self-responsibility, introduced by Ollie, stay as the useful focus for much of the session, as well as his being HIV-positive.

In the final minutes, the title The Peace Party is decided on as the group name. Jane, often contentious in manner, pushed hard for this.

In supervision, Kate criticises herself for being as directive as she was at the beginning. She and her supervisor conjecture that The Peace Party is a title that embodies the hopes of the variously troubled members, and probably some of their experience in the largely friendly and respectful second session.

Extracts from the third session: Power versus intimacy

People are sitting round the room where they always meet, talking in pairs or threes. Kate withdraws herself from one of these conversations and sits quietly as the official start time of the meeting shows on the clock. Other people begin to quieten until there is silence around the room. Many eyes turn towards her. She stays quiet. Nearly a minute passes.

Dan: Well, I want to start. [*He looks at Kate*] Is that OK?
Pat: Tom isn't here yet. [*Silence again.*]
Dan: [*to Kate, with some irritation*] I asked if it was OK to start.
Kate: I was just replaying in my mind that little scene of you asking, and me just sitting quiet. I had noticed the way people looked to me. Yes, I imagined the metaphorical meaning, you looked to me to get things going. And I remembered what my mother used to say to us as children. You're big enough and ugly enough to do that by yourselves. So I suppose the answer I never got to uttering was about reminding you of your responsibility for doing what you want. Is it OK for you to start? Who's going to say?
Pat: He was only being polite.
Jane: Gestalt begins to sound like an invitation to trample over people.
Dan: I want to start! Like, move it!
Kate: Now I'm [*She gets up and dashes between people to illustrate what she is saying*] really interested in what you and Jane are saying, Pat. And my mind

rushes back to Dan, and ideas about what he means and what we all mean by 'start'. And I'm aware of Babs not saying a word yet. And here's an empty chair where Tom will sit … [*Tom comes in at this moment.*]

Tom: Sorry I'm late. Have you started?

Dan: No.

Clare: [*simultaneously*] Yes.

This is a potentially very fruitful beginning to the evening's work. A choice for Kate now is whether to continue in the frustrating way in which she has begun. This style contrasts with her more forthcoming and encouraging openings of the earlier meetings.

She has talked before of the theory of self-responsibility. Her present enactment of it, and refusal to take overt control of the start seems already to have been followed by hostile responses from Pat, Jane and Dan. Will it be of best use to the group to focus on this, which is likely to do with what could be called the counter-dependent stage of the group? If she does, there may not be time to go through everyone's scales, and report on those and do whatever work they generate. She reflects that the members of this group see themselves here primarily to work on the issues outlined on those scales. So at this moment Kate's knowledge of small group process will perhaps best be used insofar as it looks likely to further this task, rather than as the prime focus of the group.

After a few moments in which Kate sits and cogitates to herself, she realises that in terms of Gestalt theory, she is retroflecting, turning back on herself. She voices some of what is described in the preceding paragraph.

Val: I think we should do what Kate wants us to.

Jane: Like, some pigs are more equal than others. [*She smiles and laughs as she speaks.*]

Clare: Meaning?

Kate: This sounds like a lively fight starting up. There are a lot of ways I can look at it. One is to see how it makes an opportunity for the rest of you, as well as these three, to work on noticing what you want and finding ways to achieve that.

Dan: I want to start! I want a check-in or whatever it's called, and then to do the progress monitoring.

Jane: Teacher's pet! Well, that's a neat way of avoiding trouble. Maybe you can bring Kate an apple next week. Or something a bit bigger. [*She laughs again.*]

Kate's intervention here is intended to remind everyone of their responsibility for their own experience. She wanted to cavil about Val's words, then realised that she does indeed want the group to do her programmed tasks. And she is more invested in looking for the area of learning in what is happening, that is likely to be of most use to the most people. A Utilitarian approach.

She notes too that she is stung into momentary rage by Jane's reference to *Animal Farm*. However, rather than becoming part of these individual dialogues, she looks to the larger field. For her at this moment this field seems to a great extent to have to do with dependence and its opposites, and assertive skills. She remembers how these are in one form or another in the charts of many group members, as well as being demonstrated in the way the group has opened this evening.

This extract exemplifies the group dynamics likely at this stage of the group's life, and the seat-of-the-pants leadership required. The name Peace Party is being honoured in the breach rather than the observance.

> The relation of present behaviour to the stated dominant interests of the members is usefully the foreground awareness for the therapist. Leland Bradford (1978) long ago pointed out that there is always far more material generated in a group than can ever be processed. Neglect of some phenomena is inevitable. The therapist's task is to focus on the whole alongside focusing, as need arises, on the particular.

More time was spent in this session on the struggle between rebellion and conformity, and on the racial stereotyping Dan experienced in Jane's remark about something bigger. The check-in was acrimoniously rejected by members, for lack of time. Next, the sub-group work on dominant foci was interrupted when Babs became very tearful, and Kate's help was sought. Kate interrupted all the sub-groups to ask if they wanted to go on with what they were doing, or return to the large group while she worked with Babs. They did the latter.

Babs told that her father had died the day after the last group, and his funeral was to be the day after this one. When she had been offered and had taken the sympathy of the rest, she came to the point of saying that she wanted the focus removed from her.

Kate: I remember you wrote something about wanting to get over hating to be in the public eye, that first meeting. Now you are sitting rather forward in the group, with Jane and Pat to lean on. I suggest that you let yourself go on taking comfort from them in the way you described just now. And maybe you will notice that you are still in the public eye. What would you like to do about that?

Babs: It's very kind of you two, but I think I'll go and sit over there. [*She moves to beside Tom, who blinks rapidly and barely looks at her.*]

Pat: [*derisively, to Tom*] Oh, come on, sonny Jim.

Tom: She says she wants to be private.

Babs: I could do with an arm. [*Blushing, Tom puts one around her awkwardly.*]

Pat: What's the matter with you?
Kate: Is anyone else remembering Tom's major focus?

> There is a teaching point for the BGT worker here. As large an event as the death of a near relative will inevitably swamp the foreground of a client. To ignore it or relegate it to the sidelines would be to model the very alienation many clients have come to therapy to overcome. Acknowledgement needs to be made that the focus of therapy has been changed for that person. He or she may wish to retire from the work. Or the loss may become the new focus. In a group or in individual work, the opportunity may also be there to gently comment on the ways in which the original focus reappears in the new one.

Extracts from the fourth session

The whole group except for Babs had assembled quietly by the starting time. Many of the group had little experience of death, and were chagrined at what they saw as their lack of awareness of Babs in the early part of the last session. Now the fear that she would not come to this meeting was voiced.

Clare: I went to the funeral, and she said then that she was coming along tonight.
Jane: It really seems a pity that Kate didn't find out Babs's news before the last meeting.
Kate: I'm remembering the guideline we set up in the first week, of talking directly to each other.
Jane: Well, as soon as I'd spoken I noticed that I was putting it on you, when I could just as well have asked myself.
Dan: Or, I hate to say this, we could have done what I said, and had the check-in at the beginning. That would have given her an opening.
Val: Let's start a go-round now. I'm still choked about Babs's Dad. It makes me think I'd better try and get somewhere with mine, before it's too late.

Preoccupations about fathers and their influence, and their connection to the troubles several people had brought to the group, now were voiced. Babs arrived, delayed by traffic congestion, and the group settled to a solid evening of work. There was markedly more owning of responsibility, and preparedness to listen, than last week.

Kate: [*near the end of the session*] I feel less tense in my shoulders than I did last week. I'm quiet, aware of Babs, but more peaceful than I have been until now in this group.
Clare: The gestalt completes. Isn't that what you'd say? It feels as if we've done what we needed to for now. Older and wiser, that's how we, sorry, how I, feel. Death has made us grow up.
Jane: I haven't taken any group time, and I'd like to book some for next week. I did say more than once that I wanted some.

Kate: I was aware of that. And then I saw Tom, and then Babs, become the focus of the group. I can make guesses about that. But first, do you have any?
Jane: I'm a really friendly person. But the group made me into the bad girl, for being cheeky to teacher last week. It was only fun.
Kate: That's your guess. You could check it out. [*Jane does, and two or three people admit that they chose not to notice her, but to listen to others.*]
Kate: Let's see if you ask for time next week.

Kate has not bought into Jane's booking time in the next group, but looks at the bid as evidence of Jane's style of asserting herself and competing. She deliberately frustrates, in other words, leaving an incomplete gestalt for Jane.

Context often suggests what is to be done. If a less assertive member managed to ask for time next week, Kate would more likely have checked with the rest of the group if they agreed. She would not, however, then take responsibility for making a space, but would make clear that it was up to the member to do so.

Session five: Tout comprendre, c'est tout pardonner

Jane: I don't really have anything very interesting to say.
Kate: I notice how you are sitting, slumped down a bit.
Jane: Oh, I don't want to be noticed. [*Kate recalls that Jane has put her out-of-control eating as her focus, and that she looks plumper than last week.*]
Kate: [*gently*] Jane, you are very noticeable.
Jane: Like having an elephant in the house. [*Dan laughs and Jane begins to cry.*]
Dan: Oh, I'm sorry.
Jane: You don't know how hurtful that is, having people laugh at you.
Dan: I'm really sorry. No I'm not. You said elephant, and it sounded funny. I think we're getting a bit precious here, so careful about every bloody word. I started to lose it last week, with all that balls-aching stuff about anti-oppressive and anti-discriminatory practice.
Tom: Yes, you started it, Jane, calling yourself an elephant.
Kate: [*interrupts as Jane starts to answer Tom angrily*] Two men and one woman. And I remember you being the one girl with two older brothers, Jane. Is this a familiar fight?
Jane: Yes. I started putting on weight when I was nine. They wouldn't have anything to do with me except pull faces and set people on me at school.

The two men are amazed and uneasy to see that they have begun playing parts in Jane's family, and the group assimilate this 'muddle about who is who' (Houston, 1998a: 32–8) for some minutes.

Ollie: An Irishwoman and a Trinidadian and a Brit, and they turn out to be siblings under the skin. Maybe I'm not such an outsider as I sometimes feel.
Kate: I think Jane's lucky. Fate has set up this experiment, of having the ghosts of her brothers show through Tom and Dan. And what is different now is that we can keep this as a safe emergency. There isn't a school playground with big boys lurking out there. She is grown-up. Tom and Dan are themselves,

who say they are on your side, Jane. Do you want to experiment a bit further? [*Jane agrees to.*]

Kate: If Dan or Tom agree, you could tell one of them more of what you are remembering, and maybe what you are wanting now.

Jane: I just feel murderous to both of them, honestly. I don't feel all dialogue-ish.

Kate is guided by this to suggest a projective experiment. Dialogue will come later, when Jane has dealt with her re-evoked feelings.

With their consent, Jane sculpts the two men into the taunting attitudes of her brothers, and herself into the cowering stance she felt herself in towards them as a child. Then Ollie suggests that she could do the opposite. She at once changes the sculpt, to her in the bullying mode, and them grovelling on the floor. This experiment is continued until projection has been disentangled from the real people present, and until Jane has experienced having the same stature as her brothers. Being as big as them seems to be the impetus to eating her size up.

Tom: I really want you to break the mould, and show that lot you don't have to go on being the oppressed female.

Jane: You don't sound much like my brother now.

Kate: He's not your brother. Go over and look at him and tell him so, then the same with Dan.

Jane: You're not Harry.

Kate: [*prompting*] You're not Harry, you're Tom, who wants me to break the mould.

Jane pays great attention to making this statement, and afterwards says she feels lighter and different, as if she can see men clearly for the first time. She says that in some way she was eating secretly to spite her brothers, to get something, even if they wanted to deprive her.

This episode illustrates Kate's concern to use immediacy wherever that seems useful, as in suggesting telling Dan face to face he is not her brother. At the beginning, and crucially in the writer's view, she asked Jane if she wanted to work, to continue the experiment inadvertently begun. Jane's assent is Kate's licence to make suggestions that would otherwise be an unacceptable imposition.

Some agreement or contract between therapist and client, or client and others in the group, always needs to be made before members launch off into experiments.

Ollie: You walked into another door, Flo.

Flo: Pardon? No, it was just – around the house.

Kate: It sounds as if there's another statement behind that one, Ollie.

Ollie: I wondered if someone poked you one.

Dan: Of course they did. It's a domestic. Isn't it, Flo?

Flo: No. It's not.

Dan: Well, I don't believe you.

Kate: I feel concerned at seeing your face like that, Flo. I see other people nodding. So that's where we've got to at the end of this session: people are ready to help, wanting to help. Jane asked for help and got it. I hope anyone, everyone, who needs to will ask the group for help.

In supervision Kate has aired her anxiety that Flo is being hit at home. She thinks it likely that Flo has been forbidden to say so. Now that the topic is out, she intends to return to it at the beginning of the next session.

Session five: Assertion

Dan and Flo are absent at the beginning.

Pat: I have to say this group is better without Dan. He's a loudmouth.
Jane: More airtime for you, Pat?
Clare: I'm thinking about Flo. She just clams up about her husband. Oh, I wish she was here, and I wish I'd said more last week.

The rest join in this conversation, with the same fears Kate has had. Half an hour into the session Dan and Flo arrive together. She is extremely agitated, and has new bruises on her face.

Dan: I found her in the waiting room, crying her heart out.
Clare: Your face, Flo!
Flo: I shouldn't be here. I must go. [*She moves to the door.*]
Kate: I want you to stay. [*Flo stays at the door, crying.*] You look very upset. And you are safe here. We have our understanding about confidentiality. Come and sit down and tell us what's happened.

Val and Jane go to Flo and help her into the circle. Gradually she tells that her husband has lost his job and become progressively more violent, and has said he will kill her if she lets the group see her face. Kate reflects silently that this is work for the police and social services rather than a therapy group.

Dan: Well, you're not staying there.
Flo: I've got nowhere to go.
Clare: I've got a spare room – you can stay with me.
Val: So have I.
Pat: Her husband has rights too, you know.
Clare: Oh, Pat, really!
Ollie: If you like, I'll go home with you so you can fetch your stuff.

The Blitz spirit has been evoked in all but Pat, and all except him, and Babs, who is dissuaded by the others, decide to go immediately to Flo's house, which is nearby, and load her belongings into Dan's van.

Kate: We're a group. What happens to Pat if the rest of you walk out? What happens to Babs?
Jane: Pat's to look after her and take her for a drink.

Tom: And Kate is to stay here and we'll all come back for the last half hour of the group, to report in.
Kate: It's your group.

This is a startling episode for the therapist, with control wrested from her. She could ask them to sit and talk over what to do, rather than behave with a spontaneity that verges on the impetuous. She could comment on the wresting of control. She could attempt to stop them directly.

In seconds, Kate has decided, albeit with a fast beating heart, to trust the group. There are enough of them to deal even with a drunk, should he be in the house. Jane is a social worker and likely to be aware of procedural rules. Removing Flo from her house sounds important, and takes precedence over the extensive process comment that could be made on this unfolding episode. A participant-led experiment is happening. Her conversations in supervision have helped her to be clear about the priorities.

Pat seems chastened by the duty assigned to him, and offers hesitantly to take Babs to a café or pub. She wants to stay near Kate, so the unlikely trio take the role somewhat of Greek chorus to the events they imagine unfolding elsewhere. Kate brings in the present.

Kate: It was strange to me that you were asked to take Babs for a drink, when having a drink is part of your problem, Pat.
Babs: And I could have gone with the group, you know. I'm in one piece.
Pat: You're not in touch with your spiritual needs. I'm actually surprised that Kate lets you stay in the group after something as important as your father's death.
Babs: The group's the only place I've got. The only family.
Pat: Well, that's partly why I stayed behind. They've all walked out on you as soon as something more interesting turns up.

Pat's casuistry, Babs's isolation and self-neglect, Pat's attacks on the group and on Kate's leadership, are all jostling for the foreground in Kate's mind. She takes as a warning the stirrings of impatience she feels towards Pat, and aims instead for the distress she assumes is beneath his nastiness.

Kate: Who walked out on you, Pat?
Pat: The whole lot of them, every night. I was the youngest by a long way, and my mother never let me go out and play with them. Never.

Forty minutes pass in individual work with Pat, in which he gains some insight into his bitterly critical attitude towards all authority. Twenty minutes before the official end of the group, the rest return.

Dan: We took two cars round there, and got all the stuff. We got it all, didn't we, Flo?
Flo: Yes. He wasn't there, but I was so frightened that he'd come back.
Ollie: You're shaking. [*He puts an arm around Flo and she cries.*]

Dan: I'd've loved to see his expression if he'd seen you going off with a black man. [*There is huge tension-relieving laughter at this statement.*]

Kate uses some of the remaining minutes to emphasise what an unexpected event has just happened, and to check that Flo will see a doctor, that Jane will have a word with the police, and that all of them will be available to each other by phone during the coming week. By common request and consent they add half an hour to the group time, to let Flo tell more of her story, and begin to settle a little. Kate feels that she will have a great deal to think over with her supervisor.

Session six: Consolidation

The session opened with a busy round of reporting and enquiring, centred on Flo and people's reactions to the rescue, with some vying to be the most concerned person. As well as what she said, Kate thought also that Flo was the group task for the moment, and was generating the inclusive (Schutz, 1966) feelings.

Kate: I imagine that I shall remember this group and these events for a very long time, and that most of you will too. So this is what happens in a therapy group! Let's get out your papers, if Ollie's brought them, and all of you can take turns to talk about how what you did around Flo is connected to your therapy topic.

Dan: In one way, I was the same old Dan, pushing everyone around.

Clare: We needed that. I'd love to be able to do what you and Jane did. Just taking charge when that was really needed.

Ollie: Well, you took charge when you pretty well made Flo choose your place rather than Val's. I'd move you up to 9 on your assertiveness chart there.

Jane: I know I eat to be big. And Dan's a big person to me, and it's not to do with what he weighs. [*She takes a packet of chocolate biscuits out of her bag and hands them to Dan*]. I don't need them any more.

After the major events of Babs's father's death, and Flo's flight from her husband, this session is soberly quiet and reflective. People continue to comment on their own and each other's progress on their focus issues, hence the title they decided for the session. There is considerable unpacking of racist fears and prejudices, and the changes of understanding that have happened in this field for many members during the previous two sessions.

Babs: I've often been scared of black students, and felt I just couldn't begin to understand anyone Asian. Now that awful embarrassing stuff about the family of Man, and World Village, all come to life inside me. I don't know how I'd keep going at the moment without all of you. Thank you.

Flo: And I need to say a thank you to Clare especially, and everyone.

After the session, Clare caught up with Kate on her way home, and asked if she could speak to her privately. Kate asked if this was something better talked of in the group. Clare, looking upset, said it needed to be private. Kate, with misgivings, let her talk.

Clare and Pat had been having an unconsummated affair, ended by Clare before session five, when she found that Pat had a wife in South Africa, and that he had been trying to persuade Babs into the same sort of relationship as he was having with Clare herself. As far as Kate could understand, he used talk of spirituality and Tantric sex to disguise his unacknowledged impotence.

Kate persuaded Clare that her own experience could be brought to the group. What might be going on between Babs and Pat was for either of them to deal with.

Kate's supervisor had admired her handling of session five, unorthodox though it was. Even the boundary-breaking of continuing the session after time seemed appropriate in the strange circumstances. She was less at ease that Kate had agreed to a private conversation with Clare. Kate reiterated Clare's evident distress, and admitted that she was very tired and had been caught off guard too.

The supervisor elicited that Clare was an only child, unlikely to be used to being shamed in front of siblings, but perhaps at ease with whispering to Mummy. Kate decided that, ethically and clinically tricky as this episode was, she might do something of the same kind again if provoked, though after a longer dialogue with the intending confidant.

Session seven: Sex

Kate was not confronted with what her supervisor had suggested, the possibility that she reveal the conversation between her and Clare. Clare, with evident emotion, told part of the story in the opening round of the group, omitting the sexual detail, but admitting her resentment of Pat for not revealing that he was married.

Pat: I consider all that a private matter and it is not what I came to this group for.
Dan: You came here to see how many women you could knock off.
Kate: Let's hear from Pat what he came to this group for.
Pat: There's no need. … It's on the form.
Jane: Enlarging your spirituality – wasn't that it?
Pat: I don't think there is one person in this group who has the slightest understanding of what I mean.
Dan: Au contraire, old fruit.
Kate: I'm noticing how you're looking at the wall and not at people, Pat. I'm sad that you have no sense of being understood. Jane sounded to me as if she was wanting to reach you. And when you were here with Babs and me that time, you seemed very trusting.
Dan: Well, then I'd say, 'watch it, Babs'.
Kate: [*enlarges focus*] I'm noticing Tom, who has such difficulties in approaching women, while Dan's accusing Pat of being too good at it.

Ollie: I don't know if other people too have been thinking about sexual things. I've got myself into a really frightened place, wondering if I am only homosexual after all.

After a little discussion, Kate helps them devise a conversation in pairs, in which they talk about as much of their sexual experience as they want to reveal to another group member. Kate is worried about who, if anybody, will pair with Pat. Val does so.

Back in the large group, several people tell of their sexual fantasies and aberrations.

Kate: If we were to name what's happening now, a bit the way we've named each group session, what might you come up with?
Val: I think it's to do with perspective.
Babs: Yes. Normalisation was the word in my mind. I'm so relieved to find I'm not the only person here who's a sort of sexual novice.
Ollie: And seeing that homosexual–heterosexual ambivalence in more people than me.

Ollie became the focus of a piece of work that involved Jane and Val.

Kate: Now we're almost at the end of time. I'm often the one to sum up some of what has struck me about a session. Any other volunteer today?
Val: I've said things I've never told before. That's been a lot of this session – really knowing, really telling. The growth of trust.
Kate: And latterly Pat has spoken very little.
Pat: I have not spoken at all. I've been ignored and that is the fault of the leader. It's the leader's task to help group members to speak.
Kate: So the growth of trust has not been universal. I hope you'll say what you need to next time, Pat. We've got to nine o'clock now.

Pat protested that Kate changed the time of ending when she felt like it. But already other people were getting up and talking among themselves, making clear that they were going.

Session eight: The negative

Everyone except Pat arrived on time. They began to check-in, ignoring his absence and speaking with what seemed to Kate almost exaggerated appreciation of the last session. Pat entered on this scene, barely acknowledged by other members.

Kate: Hello Pat. [*He does not reply.*]
Val: I need to speak. I feel so offended with how you spoke to Kate last week, Pat. That group was so important to me. I just feel after that that I'm not going to get all those ghastly things wrong with my vagina. Don't the rest of you feel ...? [*Signs and sounds of assent are heard. Kate feels alarm.*]
Kate: I'm noticing the polarity between Pat's experience of the group, and most other people's. I'm looking at the group as if it is an organism, and

puzzling over what is going on, that bad feelings are only being expressed by one person. The bad feelings are here, and yet no one but Pat mentions them tonight.

Pat: I consider this group quite unsuitable to have anything to do with a Primary Care Trust, and think a complaint should be made to the authorities about how it is led.

Flo: You're frightening me, Pat. You sound like my husband.

Pat: It's not the first time I've had to be the whistle-blower, and I don't enjoy it, I can tell you.

Dan: Pull the other one, darling.

Kate: You're saying that you know how to get into this position, and that you don't enjoy it. Would you like to take some time to look at that more? [*He shrugs. The rest look unenthusiastic.*] There's a lot here for all of us to learn about getting trapped into emotional positions. [*With emphasis*] I don't believe that Pat is the only one who has grudges about things that have gone on here.

Gradually people acknowledge some small criticisms and questionings about past sessions, some to do with not having enough attention when they wanted it.

Kate: I'm making a guess that you would like more attention, more respectful attention, paid to you in the whole group, Pat?

Pat: You all hear how Dan treats me. And anyway, I'm not interested in all this personal petty stuff. The transpersonal rises above all that.

Clare flushes and moves to speak, but stays quiet when Kate catches her eye. It takes most of the session to explore Pat's disastrous talent for being scapegoated and then vengeful, and the readiness of the others to form up against him. Babs recalls how Pat's father behaved, and how Kate is being tarred with the same brush.

Val: I too have my strong spiritual side, Pat, through my yoga and meditational practices. And somehow I see spirituality coming out of all these emotional harrowing experiences, not being an alternative to them.

Ollie: A sort of winnowing.

Clare: I don't feel very OK towards you yet, Pat. But I want to say that I don't see that there is anything shameful in not being, not being very, sort of potent, for sex.

Kate realises that Clare has been aware of impotence as a likely motive behind Pat's sexual practices. She also suspects that Pat may find it easier to nurse grudges than to move on.

Session nine: Chewing the cud

Tom: I've been thinking about going through everyone's scale thingummies, and about giving feedback to each other, and I think we ought to start on that now instead of leaving it all to the last session and some people being left out.

Responsibility for the group is shared. Kate is in a sense now a peer or sister, rather than the authority or mother.

Flo: So you're getting some good marks on your assertiveness chart just by saying that.
Tom: And so are you, by being cheeky. [*They laugh.*]
Val: Oh my, lovebirds. [*Babs looks disturbed.*]
Tom: No. Just good mates. [*Flo looks wistful and says nothing. Tom's idea is taken up. Val suggests that people take turns being in the limelight, and that everyone says a sentence about that person, starting 'I'.*]
Dan: The only problem I have with that is that it seems like you are taking over running this group.
Ollie: Instead of you.
Kate: I think you've learned that sort of fast answer from Dan. It's been one of his gifts to the group, or at least, to the people who wanted to be more assertive. And, Dan, Val wanted to learn more about running groups.
Dan: She won't learn if she doesn't let you be a model.

Session ten: A good end

The rest of session nine and much of the last session passed in doing the experiment Tom had suggested. This was modified as time went by, so that finally each person in the limelight had another appointed as secretary, to write down the sentences uttered by the rest. That pair then reviewed progress on the range scales, while the next in line found a secretary and came into the limelight.

In Kate's estimation, the group had cohered and become a full working entity now. Rather than compete or placate, people looked for and usually found a breadth of different comments to each person. The comments were owned as personal statements by the speakers, and accepted rather than disputed by the recipients. Concentration was high, as the shrewdness and observation of all members was made manifest. People looked pleased with themselves and each other. Pat gave some acceptable feedback to some people, had none for Dan or Clare or Babs or Kate, and refused a secretary for himself, implying that he did not value what the group would say about him.

Babs: My father was sometimes not very nice during that last year when he was so ill. I knew he might die at any time, and I thought, well, I'll make a good end with him even if he won't with me. So I lived as if every day might be his last, not soppy, but not angry inside myself. And now I'm thinking, I can make a good ending with everyone here, even if it's harder for Pat to make a good ending with us.
Pat: You're putting words in my mouth – I never said …

Val interrupted with thanks to Kate for how she had led the group. The last half hour passed in recalling the events that people had learned from during the 10 weeks, from the raid on Flo's house, through various formal experiments, to small gestures and sentences that had great meaning for different people.

Flo: I can't bear to say goodbye.
Kate: Perhaps we could do something for goodbye, rather than just say it.
Val: Lots of hugs.
Ollie: I've brought a tape of a circle dance about greeting, and parting and moving on. It's very simple to learn.

Everyone joined in. And so the group ended.

Conclusion

A great deal is left out even from this long account. This group was chosen because it demonstrates some quite unlikely events, and one BGT practitioner's way of dealing with them. There has been some necessary camouflage of identity in this account, which makes a full review of the range-scale development less than scientifically valid. It must be enough to say that all members made positive moves on their scales, in self and observer report, except Pat in the last session. Tom, Dan, Ollie and Jane made the most progress, while Clare made the least.

Pat wrote a letter of rambling complaint to the practice manager. It became clear that he had previously complained about the GP and the dentist in the practice, and sued the leader of a meditation course.

In hindsight, Kate recognised that she had reservations about Pat from the time of first meeting. But she had much the same feelings about Val and to some extent about Dan, and had attributed them to her own primitive fear and hostility in a new scene. She left herself alternately angry with Pat, sad at the life position he had, and rueful at the thought of how much group time and love had been offered to him, apparently to no effect.

Flo, Babs and Ollie asked to join the next group, in which Val was to be the apprentice assistant to Kate. In the event, Babs and Tom moved in together and she did not return to the group. The reduction in physical symptoms was marked in the women who had presented with them. Surgery attendance in the following year dropped to nil for four members, and one for three. Tom and Babs moved away and could not be traced. Dan fell off a ladder, and made several surgery visits that appear to have been unconnected to the symptoms that had taken him to the group.

Practice points

Apprenticeship is needed before leading a BGT group, unless it is done in a very programmed way. Even the programmed group, however, for people with no therapeutic experience, may be valuable.

Issues around **power** are more available to be worked with in a group than in one-to-one therapy. A progress from rivalry or compliance to functional power sharing is an ideal.

The leader will do well to have knowledge of one or two **theories of group behaviour** that she understands and believes she has seen demonstrated in other places.

Intrapsychic work may take much of the attention of individual members the first time they are in a therapy group.

There are as many groups present as people, in terms of the family and other group experience that has shaped members' expectations.

Any BGT group leader loses effectiveness unless she comments on process at **intrapersonal, interpersonal and group level**.

10

Evidence, Authority and Now in BGT

Using evidence available now

This section draws on O'Brien and Houston (2000: 26–8).

One thing is clear from research already available, and that is that therapists who practise BGT need to learn from other disciplines as well as their own.

Lambert and Bergin (1994) state that

> ... based on our review of the evidence, it appears that what can be firmly stated is that factors common across treatments are accounting for a substantial amount of improvement in psychotherapy treatments. These so-called common factors may even account for most of the gains that result from psychological interventions. (p. 163)

They suggest that therapists need to set about deliberately incorporating these factors into their treatments.

In the same way, Norcross and Newman (1992) argue that learning what is common across different approaches may lead to selecting what works best among them (p. 13). They quote Goldfried (1980):

> To the extent that clinicians of varying orientations are able to arrive at a common set of strategies, it is likely that what emerges will consist of robust phenomena, as they have managed to survive the distortions imposed by the therapists varying theoretical bias. (p. 996)

From their review of literature on the topic, Grencavage and Norcross (1990) identified four broad categories of helpful common factors in psychotherapy:

1. **Client characteristics**, such as positive expectations, hope or faith, their own distress, and their eagerness to seek help;
2. **Therapist qualities**, for example, warmth and positive regard, the cultivation of hope and positive expectation, empathic understanding, being a socially-sanctioned healer, being non-judgemental and accepting;
3. **Change processes**, like insight, catharsis, the provision of a rationale for understanding, the provision of information; plus
4. **Treatment methods**, including the use of techniques and procedure, adherence to a theory, creating a healing setting, interaction between

the two people involved, and explanation of the client and therapist roles (see Table 2, p. 82, in McLeod, 1993).

They argue that there is a development sequence in the therapy process and that factors in it can be grouped into three categories: **support factors**, **learning factors** and **action factors**.

Support factors precede learning. Learning here means changes in beliefs and attitudes. These in turn go before attempts by the therapist to encourage action, or behavioural change. They suggest that in any model, these factors operate to a greater or lesser degree as they

> provide a co-operative working endeavour in which the patient's increased trust, security and safety, along with decreases in tension, threat and anxiety, lead to changes in conceptualising his or her problems and ultimately in acting differently in interpersonal relationships. (Lambert, 1992: 104)

Here then a sequence is spelled out. Readers may well reflect that they instinctively or through training do in fact suppose the need for such a sequence, but the fact that there is research data to support their instincts is important. Gestalt dialogue is at best an expression of close attention and listening, and provides some of the support that Grencavage and Norcross (1990) have identified as a prerequisite of progress. It is arguable that good diagnostic skill, though not mentioned in the writings quoted here, will be more evidence to the client that he is in safe hands.

Diagnosis has a medical reverberation in many therapists' minds, and may sound alienating. The root meaning of the word is to do with knowing (gnosis) through (dia), which can be rendered perhaps as knowing through and through. Nobody can know another person through and through, especially at first meeting or over a short spell of therapy. **However, a diagnostic attitude, of seeking to know, by means of dialogue or talking through, is a major tool of many therapies, Gestalt among them.**

Support is also shown in BGT in the therapist's frequent recognition of the authority of the client, as the world expert on his own feelings, difficulties and wishes, for example; his ability to devise some of his own treatment again comes into the category of support, as well as what Grencavage and Norcross call learning.

In Brief Gestalt Therapy, action and learning proceed in tandem. What in Gestalt Therapy is termed the 'safe emergency' is a dry run, a rehearsal, often of new or feared behaviour. Attitudinal change may follow this action step, rather than the other way about.

Evidence, authority and now

There is a story of a civil servant who asked worriedly, 'Well, I can see that it works in practice, but will it hold up as a theory?' This quotation is not offered flippantly. There is tension, in these early years of the new millennium, between intuition and trust of the organism on the one hand, and evidence and theoretical authority on the other. The danger is of disallowing spontaneity, in favour of a kind of political correctness in constantly citing academic authority for every thought or intervention.

To disregard the growing enlightenment of new research into, for example, human motivation and behaviour, into pharmacology, neurology, therapeutic methods and clients' psychological needs, would be wasteful in the extreme. Pantheoretical research is still urgently needed into processes of mind and intersubjective processes. New co-operations will need to be made between neurologists, sociologists, psychologists and psychotherapists, to bring such a project to success.

At the same time, it is perhaps useful to remember that Copernicus guessed, correctly, that the earth moved round the sun rather than the other way about. He did so without scientific proofs, but by observing and thinking.

There is still much room for therapists to observe and think and as a result move their own theories tentatively forward. The present climate inclines people only to use the research methods that have become so respectable that they threaten to put all others out of court, and that can only be dysfunctional.

Carl Rogers (1957: 95) emphasises the need for genuineness or authenticity in the therapist, for non-judgemental acceptance of the client, and empathy. Within the client-centred model these are considered necessary and sufficient conditions for change. Kohut (1977), with his emphasis on sensitivity to the client's subjective experience, including her experience of the therapist, has much the same conviction. Sullivan required respectful empathic engagement with the client, but did not see this as necessarily enough to bring about change. All schools would agree that these important variables of the therapist's attitude are fundamental to the formation of the working alliance, and the reviewers of research are '... virtually unanimous in their opinion that the therapist–patient relationship is critical; however, they point out that research support for this position is more ambiguous than once thought' (Lambert and Bergin, 1994: 165).

What has emerged is that clients are consistently more positive in their perceptions of relationship factors than are objective observers. Correlations are higher when measures between process ratings by clients, and their self-reports of outcome, are used. For example, in a study by Miller et al. (1980), which used behavioural approaches in problem drinkers, therapists' rank on empathy correlated highly with outcome. This was a surprising result in a behavioural model, and suggests strongly that even in such a school, therapists' communicative skills are of great importance. Variations in specific technique, on the other hand, did not have a similarly powerful effect on outcome. This importance of therapists' empathy for outcome was confirmed by a more recent study by Lafferty et al. (1989).

The need and opportunities for BGT research

The research that exists is helpful but inadequate (O'Leary, 1992). This chapter sets out to encourage readers towards useful research in future BGT, as a large creative void lies before us. Much of what follows here is indeed about improving knowledge and practice for the benefit of clients, but it seems advisable to remember that there are more political aspects too. Crudely, if there is no base of evidence for the efficacy of any therapy, there is in future very unlikely to be any funding for it. In Germany, as a warning example, Gestalt Therapy is no longer given statutory funding. The obvious that needs to be stated here, and yet is sometimes disguised by researchers in other psychotherapies, is that research is by no means necessarily geared only towards clinical excellence.

The United Kingdom Council for Psychotherapy (UKCP), now heading towards statutory regulation of the profession, has a training requirement about research. This is in many places more honoured in the breach than the observance. Where it is observed, much resistance is reported by trainees.

Unfortunately, there is a good deal of unease and mystification around the whole subject of psychotherapy and research. There is a current struggle between an insistence that it be done, and exasperation with its methods, findings and feasibility (O'Brien and Houston, 2000; Roth and Fonagy, 1996). Part of this is attributable to the often huge divide between clinicians and academics. Such separation is very often associated with rivalry and hostility (Houston, 1993; Merry and Brown, 1987; Miller and Rice, 1967). Each of these groups is dependent on the other, and potentially of enormous benefit to the other. It may be that some demystification of research language, thought processes and methods, as ably begun by Avril Drummond (1996), will bring about more enthusiastic co-operation between more people from both groups.

At its simplest, research into psychotherapy and counselling can be examined according to:

1. What it is meant to show;
2. How it is conducted, by what criteria, what means and what measures;
3. Who it is meant for.

What is it meant to show?

The advancement of knowledge, and from that the enhancement of therapeutic effectiveness, by a great range of particular investigations, seems an acceptable answer to the first question. However, the baser motive of rivalry between schools of therapy can sometimes be postulated from the finding that a great deal of research is favourable to the school whose disciples carried it out. The possible outcome is the favouring by funding authorities of the school of therapy doing best in the evidence league table. So the question of whom the research is meant for creeps into the field.

How is it conducted, by what criteria, what means and what measures?

The second question leads to even thornier thickets. Randomised control tests (RCTs) are a form of research greatly favoured by some funding bodies. These RCTs are of obvious use in finding out about the efficacy of such things as drugs in the treatment of specific diseases. Is there such a thing as a sufficiently-like control group in RCTs in therapy? Can placebo therapy either exist, or be maintained, if any warmth of contact occurs between client and researcher?

Where one sort of distress is studied, as is often the case, no account is taken of comorbidity, of those other kinds of distress attendant on or alongside it. More than that, disorder, anxiety, depression and so forth, are not the sole reason for people to seek help. Many depressed, anxious, obsessional or otherwise troubled people do not seek professional help. The so-called disorder that is so often the topic of research is the foreground to a large background of unease, much of it – in the observation of many practitioners – to do with low self-worth. That in turn is connected strongly to relational difficulties.

The relational aspects of therapy – what in Gestalt is ungraciously termed the management of the contact boundary – is probably the single most significant factor in much therapy. Alongside and following that come the techniques, most of which are unlikely to be of help where there is no trusting contact.

Tyson and Range (1987) possibly elicited evidence of this in their Gestalt experiments with mildly-depressed patients. They used the same therapist to do empty-chair work, neutral dialogue, attention placebo and strong affect encounters with 44 subjects arranged in four treatment groups. The reduction in depression and maintenance after two months was similar in all groups. It is tempting to suppose that researcher rather than method altered those researched, since the researcher was the only apparent constant.

Gestalt stresses the subjective nature of experience. There is room to honour this emphasis, by qualitative research alongside quantitative studies such as those described in this book.

Who is it meant for?

If research is aimed at funding agencies, then the lesson from other schools of therapy is that it will best be directed to showing that the treatment under scrutiny is highly successful. This statement is intended as advice, not as cynicism. Most therapies are highly successful, within defined parameters. BGT is successful over a wide field, and deserves to have this fact revealed in scientific studies.

If research is primarily directed at improving the service offered to clients, different questions emerge. In such research, therapists or researchers can focus in two major ways. One is to identify those aspects of the therapy that are consistently efficacious. The other is to search out those aspects that tend to detract from efficacy. Both have great importance, and are of value both to BGT therapists, and to the whole field of improving psychotherapy.

It should not be forgotten or overlooked that every therapist who works at self-improvement, in the cause of doing as well as possible for the client, is a researcher. We ceaselessly note the apparent effects on clients of ourselves, our words and attitudes. We draw conclusions, form hypotheses, experiment with new or reinforced interventions, and watch the outcome. This sort of evidence gathering and reflection is often only talked about in supervision, or at some moments to the clients themselves. It is potentially or actually valuable. But it is small, private, not subject to much comparison, incapable of statistical analysis, and so seems not to count formally as evidence.

The encouraging fact is that BGT practitioners are often fortunate in terms of quantitative research, in that they tend to see large numbers of people, often for a set number of sessions. If the range scales suggested in this book are used, these will of themselves produce a large body of data. Brief Gestalt therapists may start from this database to experiment with small pieces of research. Having the therapist score progress on the same constructs at the same time as the client is one possible extension. Having a friend and/or family member do similarly produces more observations still. A follow-up session after the main episode of therapy gives an opportunity for longitudinal study.

This is one small example of how evidence can be generated, in a way that may be of immediate interest and benefit to the client, as well as longer-term benefit to the therapist, the profession and general clinical practice.

Training and evidence gathering

Lack of evidence does not necessarily mean lack of effectiveness. But humility and a spirit of enquiry should encourage practitioners to find ways of moving their possibly-shrewd clinical observations into a larger testing ground than their own experiences with a small number of people. The challenge is there for trainers to waken students to the excitement of finding ways to form and test hypotheses, in a way that educates them to incorporate research into their work for the rest of their careers.

Galileo's father Vincenzio wrote:

> It appears to me that they who in proof of any assertion rely simply on the weight of authority, without adducing any argument in support of it, act very absurdly. I, on the contrary, wish to be allowed freely to question and freely to answer you without any sort of adulation, as well becomes those who are in search of truth. (Galilei, 1581)

Like his son, he was a scientific iconoclast. Fritz Perls and other Gestalt thinkers were in the same tradition, and it is one we do well to preserve. Before Vincenzio wrote the statement quoted here, he had laboured hard to translate the Pythagorean rule of musical ratios into a tuning formula that involved slightly shortening the spaces between the frets on the lute. In other words, he took a fresh look at reality, and in the light of new awareness, made changes in structure and practice.

The phenomenological method at the heart of Gestalt Therapy is of itself a fresh look at reality.

> Husserl argued that it was necessary to examine the bedrock of everyday experience, because it was there, in our emotions, actions and perceptions of things and relationships, that an ultimately true experience could be derived. Phenomenology strives to describe the *essence* of everyday experience. (McLeod, 2001: 37)

Phenomenology can be described perhaps as a right-hemispheric approach to truth. It needs to encompass co-created reality, the between, rather than any rigidly-maintained personal construct. That is a ticklish matter to research by many quantitative methods.

Areas for BGT research

O'Leary (1992: 120) identifies what she sees as priorities in Gestalt Therapy research. These include replication studies, the development of reliable and valid measures of constructs employed in Gestalt Therapy, investigations that consider process and outcomes simultaneously, and studies that examine various aspects of emotion. The use of randomisation, both in the selection of subjects and in their assignment into treatments, has been highlighted. Finally, when analysing and studying findings, it is vital to use appropriate statistical methods in order to ensure that the maximum information gain is achieved. Pushing ahead with innovative practice, allowing oneself to be influenced by qualitative research based on experience, should never allow us to be blind to the value of more rigorous and quantitative findings of academic researchers.

BGT is indeed one of the therapies that lends itself to quantitative research. It can generate a great deal of data, at the least, for outcome studies. Evidence of good outcome is the feedback loop required by any therapist who pays attention to what she is doing. Outcome research is implicit in the BGT system described in this book. It will be strengthened by follow-up at some months, as suggested.

Where another session can be built in at six months or a year, the therapeutic impact is often enhanced, and the outcome data enlarged in a useful way. In Primary Health Care settings, where much BGT is practised, access to former clients is often easier than elsewhere, so a dossier of longitudinal evidence can be built up through the longer contact available.

Invention and play in research

Along with the innovations in therapy that each generation will make, are needed innovations in research methods. The students of artificial intelligence, who predicted that by 2001 a conscious robot such as HAL would be trotting about creating mayhem, have revised their notions. They admit now that the human mind is vastly more powerful, subtle and variable than they had assumed.

This complexity suggests that it will continue to be massively difficult to find ways of researching and ways of usefully measuring and comparing different therapies. For example, 'it ain't what you say, it's the way that you say it'. One therapist will engage enhancingly and effectively with a client. She may do poorly with another. Or a therapist from the same school may turn out to be of little apparent use to the same client, though she makes apparently similar interventions.

At a UKCP conference on evidence-based practice in 2001, Peter Fonagy encouraged clinicians to be playful with research. By this, I think he meant that we should let ourselves be inventive and exploratory without obsessional regard for statistical reliability and many other proper academic concerns. Where video is allowable and appropriate in BGT, there is a potential for some of this playful research, that at best will lead to the eliciting of much dependable evidence. Perls (1969) advised:

> Don't listen to the words, just listen to what the words tell you, what the movements tell you, what the posture tells you.... The sounds tell you everything ... the voice is there, the gesture, the posture, the facial expression, the psychosomatic language. (p. 57)

If observation of all this is undertaken, alongside subjective reporting, much may be learned (Izard, 1968).

What makes our profession so tantalising, challenging and rewarding is largely what makes it quicksilver to many research methods: no client or group clones another. So the use of controls is less telling in therapy research than in pharmacological trials, for example. Yet on the one hand, academics chide clinicians for not using control groups, while clinicians sometimes deride all research into therapy as worthless. Neither position is helpful to the advancement of learning.

The introduction of range scales suggested in this book leads to a kind of process–outcome research that has value for the client as well as the researcher. In psychotherapy, this dimension of awareness of what is of direct use to the client or group under scrutiny should, in the opinion of the writer, be the priority in most studies. In particular, any quantitative studies should in most cases be based on this requirement.

In BGT it is not difficult to ask clients to fill out a multiple-choice questionnaire on their sense of the therapist and feelings towards her, alongside their own assessment of the therapeutic progress they have made.

When clients are asked what they have found most helpful, they usually mention common rather than specific factors (Llewelyn and Hume, 1979). Interestingly, Strupp and Hadley (1979) argue that non-specific factors and therapeutic relationship are one and the same. They found no significant difference between trained therapists using specific techniques and empathic but untrained university tutors asked to act as 'counsellors' (Strupp and Hadley, 1979). They attributed the results and the positive changes in clients, in both the expert and non-expert groups, to the healing effects of benign human relationship (p. 1135).

In his book *Persuasion and Healing*, Frank (1973) looked at similarities between psychotherapy, placebo effects in medicine, brainwashing and faith healing, in our Western culture and in others. He suggests that all psychotherapies are variations of ancient routes to psychological healing. They deal with a common problem of demoralisation. This includes loss of self-esteem, alienation, a subjective sense of incompetence, hopelessness and helplessness. He believes that the common task of all therapy is the restoration of morale, and he sees little difference between different therapies in achieving this task (Norcross and Arkowitz, 1996).

Implications for research

> … doing good qualitative research is not merely a matter of following a set of procedural guidelines. The principal source of knowing in qualitative inquiry is the researcher's engagement in a search for meaning and truth in relation to the topic of inquiry. It is the struggle to know that generates new and useful insights. (McLeod, 2001: 54)

The current emphasis on evidence-based practice risks encouraging partisan qualitative research, that appears to prove the efficacy of whatever approach is being examined. McLeod makes a convincing case for the combination of **phenomenology** and **hermeneutics**, if good qualitative research in psychotherapy is to be done. To achieve this, he argues that therapists need to return to the philosophical roots of the approaches they use.

Husserl advocated a phenomenology that was a great deal more than recounting personal response to any event. He was interested in moving towards the essence of experience, and exploring the outer edges of what language can convey. It is salutary to read Sass's (1988) criticism of Husserl. He suggests that Husserl's phenomenology leads to such a reliance on idiosyncratic personal experience that our social nature is denied.

Much of this chapter has been about hermeneutics, the collating of data concerning different culture-bound assumptions, so that a possibly enlightening fusion is obtained. Insofar as phenomenology can be seen as a right-brain epistemology, so hermeneutics depends more on rational, left-hemisphere work. For Gestalt to sacrifice phenomenology to hermeneutics would be a methodological and philosophical loss. Heidegger (see Moran, 2000) is perhaps the philosopher to restore hope here. In shorthand, where Husserl sought to get away from ordinary assumptions, or what he called natural attitude, Heidegger was clear that it was the true nature of the everyday, the natural attitude, that could lead to an appreciation of the phenomenological essence (1962).

Heidegger (1962) used ideas from both epistemologies, in an attempt to understand existence itself. However dubiously he himself applied his method in his life, his approach can inform present research into Brief Gestalt Therapy. This is in some ways a new conception or construct, which arguably makes it amenable to a fresh examination. Such assumptions, as that longer is better in therapy, are not fully corroborated by hermeneutic methods of enquiry. As long ago as 1946, Alexander and French, quoted in O'Connell (1998: 1), spoke of the 'almost superstitious belief among psychoanalysts that quick therapeutic results cannot be genuine'.

When there is a carefully-recorded phenomenology of BGT, garnered from the experience of practitioners and clients, this may lead even to a re-evaluation of long-term therapy itself.

Conclusion

Research is in modern times very often highly political in effect and in intention, but that does not mean that it is not important. It is to be noted that alertness to the operations of power is emphasised in this therapy. BGT is alive and flourishing. Research studies are urgently needed, and beginning to be undertaken, to demonstrate the value of both its integrity and its integrative power.

Practice points

The direction in which BGT tends is congenial to qualitative and quantitative research. It is important that BGT practitioners have a **researchful attitude**, looking for evidence to back or disprove their observations and hunches.

De-construction of many assumptions about what constitute valid instruments of research is needed. De-construction is the work of Gestalt.

Inventiveness of method is central to our practice, and is greatly needed if research is to stay appropriate to the subject and purpose of enquiry. Effectiveness is the key to good practice, and transcends orthodoxy as a criterion.

Absence of evidence does not necessarily mean lack of effectiveness. It does mean lack of academic and economic power. Only with these powers can BGT be recognised and brought into the wide practice it merits.

References

Avery, A. (1999) 'Letter to *British Gestalt Journal*', *British Gestalt Journal*, 8 (1): 55.

Beisser, A. (1970) 'The paradoxical theory of change', in J. Fagan and I. Shepherd (eds), *Gestalt Therapy Now*. Palo Alto, CA: Science and Behavior Books.

Bion, W. (1961) *Experiences in Groups*. London: Tavistock.

Bloom, B.L. (1992) *Planned Short-term Psychotherapy*. Boston, MA: Allyn and Bacon.

Bradford, L. (ed.) (1978) *Group Development*. La Jolla, CA: University Associates.

Bradford, L.P., Gibb, J.R. and Benne, K.D. (1964) *T-Group Theory and Laboratory Method*. New York: John Wiley.

Buber, M. (1970) *I and Thou*. New York: Scriveners.

Burton, M. (1998) *Psychotherapy, Counselling and Primary Mental Health Care*. Chichester: John Wiley and Sons.

Casement, P. (1985) *On Learning From the Patient*. London: Tavistock.

Clarke, K.M. and Greenberg, L.S. (1986) 'Differential effects of the Gestalt two-chair intervention and problem-solving in resolving decisional conflict', *Journal of Counselling Psychology*, 53 (1): 11–15.

Clarkson, P. (1989) *Gestalt Counselling in Action*. London: Sage.

Conoley, C.W., Conoley, J.C., McConnell, J.A. and Kimzey, C.G. (1983) 'The effects of ABCs of rational-emotive therapy and the empty-chair technique of Gestalt therapy on anger reduction', *Psychotherapy: Theory, Research and Practice*, 20 (2): 112–17.

Curwen, B., Palmer, S. and Ruddell, P. (2000) *Brief Cognitive Behaviour Therapy*. London: Sage.

da Vinci, Leonardo (1952) *Notebooks of Leonardo da Vinci*. Edited by I.A. Richter. London: OUP.

Darwin, C. (1872) *The Expression of the Emotions*. London: Folio Edition 1990.

Department of Health (2001) 'Treatment choice in psychological therapies and counselling'. Pamphlet ref. 23454.

Drummond, A. (1996) *Research Methods for Therapists*. London: Chapman and Hall.

Eliot, T.S. (1944) *The Four Quartets*. London: Faber and Faber.

Evans, K. (1999) 'Brief and focal Gestalt therapy in a group', *British Gestalt Journal*, 8 (1): 15–18.

Fairbairn, W.R.D. (1952) *An Object Relations Theory of Personality*. Boston, MA: Routledge and Kegan Paul.

Fisch, R. and Schlanger, K. (1998) *Brief Therapy with Intimidating Cases: Changing the Unchangeable*. Chichester: Wiley.

Flegenheimer, W.V. (1982) *Techniques of Brief Psychotherapy*. New York: Jason Aronson.

Frank, J.D. (1973) *Persuasion and Healing: A Comparative Study of Psychotherapy*. Baltimore, MD: Johns Hopkins University Press.

Frew, J. (1992) 'Three styles of therapeutic intervention'. Lecture at the International Gestalt Conference, Boston, MA.

Friedman, M. (1990) 'Dialogue philosophical anthropology and Gestalt therapy', *The Gestalt Journal*, 13 (1): 7–40.

From, I. (1984) 'Reflections on Gestalt therapy after thirty two years of practice: a requiem for Gestalt', *The Gestalt Journal*, 7 (1): 4–12.

Fuhr, R., Sreckovic, M. and Gremmler-Fuhr, M. (2000) 'Diagnostics in Gestalt Therapy', *Gestalt Review*, 4 (3): 238.

Galilei, V. (1581) 'Dialogo sulla musica ancient e moderna', in F. Antonio (ed.) (1909), *Edizione Nazionale delle opere di Galileo Galilei*. Rome: Universita di Roma.

Gallese, V. and Goldman, A. (1998) 'Mirror neurons and the simulation theory of mind-reading', *Trends in Cognitive Sciences*, 2 (2): 493.

Gleick, J. (1988) *Chaos*. Harmondsworth: Viking Penguin.

Goldfried, M.R. (1980) 'Towards a delineation of therapeutic change principles', *American Psychologist*, 35: 991–9.

Goldfried, M.R. (ed.) (1982) *Converging Themes in Psychotherapy: Trends in Psychodynamic, Humanistic and Behavioural Practice*. New York: Springer.

Goldstein, K. (1939) *The Organism*. Boston, MA: American Book Co.

Grencavage, L.M. and Norcross, J.C. (1990) 'Where are the commonalities among the therapeutic common factors?', *Professional Psychotherapy: Research and Practice*, 21: 371–8.

Havens, L.L. (1986) *Making Contact: Uses of Language in Psychotherapy*. Cambridge, MA: Harvard University Press.

Hawkins, P. and Shohet, R. (2000) *Supervision in the Helping Professions*. Buckingham: Open University Press.

Heidegger, M. (1962) *Being and Time*. Oxford: Blackwell.

Houston, G. (1993) *Being and Belonging: Group, Intergroup and Gestalt*. Chichester: John Wiley.

Houston, G. (1995) *Supervision and Counselling*. London: Rochester Foundation.

Houston, G. (1998a) *The New Red Book of Gestalt*, third edition. London: Rochester Foundation.

Houston, G. (1998b) *The Red Book of Groups*, second edition. London: Rochester Foundation.

Husserl, E. (1960) *Cartesian Meditations: An Introduction to Phenomenology*. Translated by Dorion Cairns. The Hague: Nijhoff.

Hycner, R.A. (1990) 'The I–Thou relationship and Gestalt therapy', *The Gestalt Journal*, 13 (2): 41–54.

Izard, C.E. (1968) 'The emotions and emotional constructs in personality and cultural research', in R.B. Cattel (ed.), *Handbook of Modern Personality Theory*. Chicago, IL: Aldine.

Jacques, G. (1999) 'Temporality in Gestalt therapy', *British Gestalt Journal*, 8 (1): 24–30.

Keenan, B. (1993) *An Evil Cradling*. London: Vintage.

Kempler, W. (1973) *Principles of Gestalt Family Therapy*. Oslo: A.J. Nordahls Trykerri.

Kepner, E. (1980) 'Gestalt group process', in B. Feder and R. Ronall (eds), *Beyond the Hot Seat – Gestalt Approaches to Group*. New York: Brunner/Mazel.

Klerman, G., Weissmann, M., Rounsaville, B. and Chevron, E. (1984) *Interpersonal Therapy for Depression*. New York: Basic Books.

Kohut, H. (1977) *The Restoration of the Self*. New York: International Universities Press.

Kolk, B. van der, McFarlane, A. and Weisaeth, L. (1996) *Traumatic Stress: The Overwhelming Experience on Mind, Body and Society*. New York: Guilford Press.

Lafferty, P., Beutler, L.E. and Crago, M. (1989) 'Differences between more or less effective therapists: a study of select therapists' variables', *Journal of Consulting and Clinical Psychology*, 57: 76–80.

Lambert, M.J. (1992) 'Psychotherapy outcome research: implications for integrative and eclectic therapies', in J.C. Norcross and M.R. Goldfried (eds), *Handbook of Psychotherapy Integration*. New York: Basic Books.

Lambert, M.J. and Bergin, A.E. (1994) 'The effectiveness of psychotherapy', in A.E. Bergin and M.J. Lambert (eds), *Handbook of Psychotherapy and Behaviour Change*. New York: John Wiley.

Latner, J. (1982) 'The thresher of time: on love and freedom in Gestalt therapy', *The Gestalt Journal*, 5 (2): 20–38.

Latner, J. (1995) 'Love in Gestalt therapy – a reply to Staemmler', *British Gestalt Journal*, 4 (1): 49–50.

Lewin, K. (1951) *Field Theory in Social Science*. New York: Harper and Row.

Llewelyn, S. and Hume, W. (1979) 'The patient's view of therapy', *British Journal of Medical Psychology*, 52 (3): 29–36.

Maibaum, M. (1992) 'A Lewinian taxonomy of psychiatric disorders'. Address to the Fifth International Kurt Lewin Conference, University of Philadelphia, PA.

Malan, D. (1982) 'The frontier of brief psychotherapy', in W. Flegenheimer (ed.), *Techniques of Brief Psychotherapy*. New York: Jason Aronson Inc.

Mander, G. (2000) *A Psychodynamic Approach to Brief Therapy*. London: Sage.

Maslow, A.M. (1956) *Towards a Psychology of Being*. New York: Van Nostrand.

McGregor, D. (1960) *The Human Side of Enterprise*. New York: McGraw-Hill.

McHugh, P. and Slavney, P. (1986) *The Perspectives of Psychiatry*. Baltimore, MD: Johns Hopkins University Press.

McLeod, J. (1993) *An Introduction to Counselling*. Buckingham: Open University Press.

McLeod, J. (2001) *Qualitative Research in Counselling and Psychotherapy*. London: Sage.

Melnick, J. and Nevis, S. (1992) 'Diagnosis: the struggle for a meaningful paradigm', in E. Nevis (ed.), *Gestalt Therapy*. New York: Gardner Press.

Mercier, M.A. and Johnson, M. (1984) 'Representational system predicate use and convergence in counselling: Gloria revisited', *Journal of Counselling Psychology*, 31 (1): 161–9.

Merry, U. and Brown, G. (1987) *The Neurotic Behaviour of Organisations*. New York: Gardner Press.

Miller, E. and Rice, A. (1967) *Systems of Organization*. London: Tavistock.

Miller, M.V. (1999) 'Introduction', in F.S. Perls, *Gestalt Therapy Verbatim*. New York: Gardner Press.

Miller, W.R., Taylor, C.A. and West, J.C. (1980) 'Focussed versus broad-spectrum behaviour therapy for problem drinkers', *Journal of Consulting and Clinical Psychology*, 48: 590–601.

Moran, D. (2000) *Introduction to Phenomenology*. London: Routledge.

Moreno, J.L. (1946) *Psychodrama*. New York: Random House.

Moreno, J.L. (1953) *Who Shall Survive? Foundations of Sociometry, Group Psychotherapy and Sociodrama*. New York: Beacon House.

Myers, D. (2000) 'The funds, friends and faith of happy people', *American Psychologist*, 55 (1): 56–67.

Nevis, E. (1987) *Organizational Consulting: A Gestalt Approach*. Cleveland, OH: Gestalt Institute of Cleveland Press.

Newberg, A., d'Aquili, E. and Rause, V. (2001) *Why God Won't Go Away*. London: Ballantine Books.

Norcross, J.C. and Arkowitz, H. (1996) 'The evolution and current status of psychotherapy integration', in W. Dryden (ed.), *Integrative and Eclectic Therapy: A Handbook*. Buckingham: Open University Press.

Norcross, J.C. and Newman, C.F. (1992) 'Psychotherapy integration: setting the context', in J.C. Norcross and M.R. Goldfried (eds), *Handbook of Psychotherapy Integration*. New York: Basic Books.

O'Brien, M. and Houston, G. (2000) *Integrative Therapy: A Practitioner's Guide.* London: Sage.
O'Connell, B. (1998) *Solution-focused Therapy.* London: Sage.
O'Leary, E. (1992) *Gestalt Therapy: Theory, Practice and Research.* London: Chapman and Hall.
Parlett, M. and Hemming, J. (1996) 'Developments in Gestalt Therapy', in W. Dryden (ed.), *Developments in Psychotherapy: Historical Perspectives.* London: Sage.
Paul, G.L. (1967) 'Strategy of outcome research in psychotherapy', *Journal of Consulting Psychology*, 31 (2): 109–18.
Perls, F.S. (1947) *Ego, Hunger and Aggression.* London: Allen and Unwin.
Perls, F.S. (1969) *Gestalt Therapy Verbatim.* New York: Real People Press.
Perls, F.S. (1973) *The Gestalt Approach and Eye Witness to Therapy.* Palo Alto, CA: Science and Behavior Books.
Perls, F.S. (1992) *Ego, Hunger and Aggression: A Revision of Freud's Theory and Method.* Highland, NY: Gestalt Journal Press.
Perls, F.S., Hefferline, R. and Goodman, P. (1951) *Gestalt Therapy: Excitement and Growth in the Human Personality.* New York: Julian Press.
Philippson, P. (1999) 'A process focus and the here and now in Brief Gestalt Therapy', *British Gestalt Journal*, 8 (1): 4–8.
Polster, E. (1987) *Every Person's Life is Worth a Novel.* New York: Norton.
Polster, E. (1991) 'Tight therapeutic sequences', *British Gestalt Journal*, 1 (2): 63–8.
Polster, E. (1993) 'Individuality and communality', *British Gestalt Journal*, 2 (1): 41–3.
Popper, K. (1972) *Conjectures and Refutations: The Growth of Scientific Knowledge.* London: Routledge and Kegan Paul.
Proust, M. (2000) *Within a Budding Grove.* London: Folio Society. Originally published 1919.
Rogers, C. (1957) 'The necessary and sufficient conditions of therapeutic personality change', *Journal of Consulting Psychology*, 21 (1): 95–103.
Rogers, C. (1961) *On Becoming a Person.* London: Constable.
Rosenthal, H.G. (ed.) (2001) *Favourite Counselling and Therapy Homework Assignments.* London: Brunner-Routledge.
Roth, A. and Fonagy, P. (1996) *What Works for Whom? A Critical Review of Psychotherapy Research.* New York: Guilford Press.
Sartre, J.P. (1956) *Being and Nothingness: An Essay on Phenomenological Ontology.* Translated by H. Barnes. New York: Philosophical Library.
Sass, L.A. (1988) 'Humanism, hermeneutics, and the concept of the human subject', in S.B. Messer, L.A. Sass and R.L. Woolfolk (eds), *Hermeneutics and Psychological Theory: Interpretive Perspectives on Personality, Psychotherapy and Psychopathology.* New Brunswick, NJ: Rutgers University Press.
Satir, V. (1972) *Peoplemaking.* Palo Alto, CA: Science and Behavior Books.
Saver, J. and Rabin, J. (1997) 'The neural substrates of religious experience', *The Journal of Neuropsychiatry*, 9: 498.
Schutz, W. (1966) *The Interpersonal Underworld.* Palo Alto, CA: Science and Behavior Books.
Scott, J. (1999) 'The ending is in the beginning', *British Gestalt Journal*, 8 (1): 19–23.
Skynner, R. (1993) Address to Royal Society of Arts. London: John Adam House.
Stern, D. (1985) *The Interpersonal World of the Infant.* New York: Basic Books.
Strupp, H.H. and Hadley, S.W. (1979) 'Specific vs. non-specific factors in psychotherapy: a controlled study of outcome', *Archives of General Psychiatry*, 36: 1125–36.
Sullivan, H.S. (1954) *The Psychiatric Interview.* New York: W.W. Norton.

Talmon, M. (1990) *Single Session Therapy*. San Francisco, CA: Jossey-Bass.

Tansella, M. and Thornicroft, G. (eds) (1999) *Common Mental Disorders in Primary Care*. London: Routledge.

Thorne, B. (1999) 'The move towards Brief Therapy: its dangers and its challenges', *Counselling*, 10 (3): 1–7.

Tyson, G.M. and Range, L.M. (1987) 'Gestalt dialogues as a treatment for mild depression: time works just as well', *Journal of Clinical Psychology*, 43 (2): 227–31.

Vevers, J. and Hemming, A. (1995) 'Gestalt groups with general practice patients: using Repertory Grid'. Unpublished research paper.

Wessler, R.L. and Wessler, S.H. (1997) 'Counselling and society', in S. Palmer and V. Varma (eds), *The Future of Counselling and Psychotherapy*. London: Sage.

Whines, J. (1999) 'Contact, field-conditions and the symptom-figure', *British Gestalt Journal*, 8 (1): 10.

Winnicott, D.W. (1959) *Collected Papers: Through Paediatrics to Psychoanalysis*. London: Tavistock.

Yontef, G. (1993) *Awareness, Dialogue and Process: Essays on Gestalt Therapy*. Highland, NY: Gestalt Journal Press.

Zinker, J. (1977) *Creative Processes in Gestalt Therapy*. New York: Brunner-Mazel.

Index